Children Without Justice:

A Report by the National Council of Jewish Women

Written by Edward Wakin

1975

National Council of Jewish Women, Inc.
One West 47th Street
New York, New York 10036

TABLE OF CONTENTS

National Council of Jewish Women, Inc.
One West 47th Street
New York, New York 10036

Foreword
By William O. Douglas

Years ago I talked with an outstanding Juvenile Court judge in one of our western States and heard him explain what I think was the original purpose of the juvenile delinquency acts of the various States. "I, the judge," he told me, "and the bailiff and the other court attendants are like those on a hospital staff, dressed in white. We are doctors, nurses, orderlies. We are there not to administer a law in the normal meaning of criminal law. We are there to diagnose, investigate, counsel and advise. We are specialists in search of ways and means to correct conduct and to help reorient wayward youngsters to a life cognizant of responsibilities to the community."

That was the true attitude in the beginning. Indeed in the early years juvenile proceedings were treated as being "civil," not "criminal" in nature. In that posture they were able to avoid all provisions of the Bill of Rights dealing with criminal procedure. But the legal minds overworked the analogy to "civil" suits and began taking short cuts. In time, treatment equivalent to criminal sanctions was being imposed without the constitutional safeguards of criminal procedure.

The only entity mentioned in the Constitution or Bill of Rights is a "person". One is a "person" at least from the moment of birth. If a "person" is to be convicted, jailed, or otherwise punished, all of the procedures applicable to adults are equally applicable to children. In time that idea took hold and three classic decisions were rendered: *Kent* v. *United States*, 383 U.S. 541, decided in 1966; *In Re Gault*, 387 U.S. 1, in 1967; and *In Re Winship*, 397 U.S. 358, in 1970. The two latter ones were constitutional decisions holding that the child was entitled to due protection at the delinquency hearing (a) by receiving adequate notice of the charges, (b) by being given the right to counsel, (c) by being accorded the protection of the guarantee against self-incrimination, (d) by having the right to confront and cross-examine witnesses, and (e) by being given the protection of proof beyond a reasonable doubt—all safeguards of the Bill of Rights made applicable to the States by reason of the Fourteenth Amendment. The Court has stopped short, however, of holding that all juvenile court procedures must be assimilated to constitutional criminal safeguards. See *McKeiver* v. *Pennsylvania*, 403 U.S. 528. Numerous perplexing questions remain unresolved, one of them being double jeopardy. When a juvenile has been adjudged a ward of the court and later is found to be unamenable to rehabilitation and remitted to the prosecutor for trial as a bank robber, does his robbery trial as an adult place him twice in jeopardy? See *Jones* v. *Breed*, 497 F. 2d 1160.

The constitutional contours of the problem have not yet been fully drawn. Important as that process may be, a court is not the medium where the problems of juvenile delinquency will ultimately be solved. The solutions can emerge only from the community, as this energizing volume illustrates. The solution is in part prevention, in part rehabilitation. Many times the parents are the real "delinquents," working cleverly to shun confrontation with their own problems and with those of the child. Spiritual, emotional abandonment of children is commonplace; all too often, it emerges as an ulcer in the familial relationship.

We must as a people look to community participation; to neighborhood awareness; and to regimes of help and surveillance that lean on people other than parents and police. China may offer some clues. That nation is highly organized. Street committees represent perhaps two square blocks. Under a street committee is a residential committee supervising a smaller segment. Under it in turn is a residential group embracing ten to fifteen families. They are not spies but collaborators. They counsel and advise, supervising and interacting with both parents and children. Their techniques are informal, suggestive, *ad hoc*. If a lad is in the toils of the police or a magistrate, it is with this local group that the official deals. If there is a parole, it may be to that group—or a group in a factory or in a commune close to the home of the child.

The Chinese approach is suggestive of possibilities here. Of course, institutions cannot be transplanted intact from one culture to another with prospects of success. Indeed, community participation with a distinct American design might vary in method from state to state. It is nevertheless at that level, not at the legal level, that progress will be made.

Institutions have a habit of growing in size and tenacity. Getting free of their toils becomes nearly impossible. They tend to crush the individual. Ideally our task should be organizing the neighborhood—the grass roots—so that there is an identifiable group of responsive and responsible people whose aim is not living for themselves but living for others. We will in time discover that that is the only path to self-fulfillment.

Acknowledgment

The original working title of this book was "2,000,000 Children: Unequal Before the Law." That staggering figure represents the number of children who are arrested each year. Subsequently, when the manuscript was completed, the title was changed. It occurs to me that the process of change is a distinguishing characteristic of National Council of Jewish Women. It has always been so.

Publication of this book is an event in which women, especially Council women, can take great pride and even greater satisfaction. This report is so much more than an accumulation of data, even though the data is often searingly dramatic. The entire project is a demonstration of how a volunteer organization acquired knowledge of a complex branch of society's judicial system; how the organization through its component member groups then began to work with the system and, when necessary, against it.

Some 3,000 Council women representing 123 Sections in 34 states and the District of Columbia, participated in this year-long study of the juvenile justice system in their communities. The survey was no mere sampling; it was a penetrating examination of one of our most basic and most vital democratic institutions, and its effect on those it was created to serve: children and society. Two very startling basic facts emerged: First, most citizens, even those who have been active in their communities, do not concern themselves with the problems and issues of our juvenile justice system. Second, most communities do not deal adequately with the needs of either children in trouble or their families.

It was the juxtaposition of NCJW's traditional concern for the needs of children and an equally compelling concern for the rights of children that provided the motivating force for the survey and that has since energized a broad range of Section activity.

I believe that a great measure of admiration is due to these women who were willing to delve into a system which was closed to the general community, in fact, to most of society. And much admiration is due them for their readiness to study, to learn, and to develop experience so that they could be helpful, not just in one area, not just in a particular project, but in the context of the entire system. Council women acquired experience and knowledge from the survey and used it to great advantage to help improve and change a system which was resistant to change.

In undertaking this examination, NCJW accepted certain challenges, faced certain risks. Juvenile justice was not a popular field. At the outset, Sections had to deal with resistance from the system on the one hand and with the community's stereotype of children behind bars on the other.

In the end, the risks were overcome. The women who participated in the study showed their deep concern for the needs of children by becoming advocates for the children. Moreover, they earned the respect of the professionals within the system.

A debt of gratitude is expressed to the members

Acknowledgment

of the Task Force on Justice for Children who have been with the program from its inception through each stage of expanding Section activity. Let me thank:

Justice For Children Task Force

Flora Rothman, Chairwoman	Gr. Flushing, (N.Y.) Section
Martha Bernstein, Vice Chairwoman	New York, (N.Y.) Section
Marjorie Horowitz	Gr. Westfield, (N.J.) Section
Dorothy Lasday	Richmond, (Va.) Section
Elaine Lederer	Fairlawn, (N.J.) Section
Dianne Leventhal	Gr. Red Bank, (N.J.) Section
Bea Rich	Rockland County, (N.Y.) Section
Paula Rosenblum	Teaneck, (N.J.) Section
Gladys Sandak	Gr. Westfield, (N.J.) Section
Evelyn Sosower	Teaneck, (N.J.) Section
June Thalheimer	Gr. Plainfield, (N.J.) Section
Ruth Zalaznick	Teaneck, (N.J.) Section

Community Activities Committee

Hortense Tonner, Chairwoman	Peninsula, N.Y.
Marilyn Shubin, Vice Chairwoman	Atlanta, Ga.

Staff

Phyllis Ross
Lois Whitman

In addition to the dedicated women who have manifested a special commitment to justice for children, I take this opportunity to express on behalf of the entire membership of NCJW, the warmest appreciation to the Greater New Orleans and Portland, Oregon Sections for their most generous gifts, which made this book possible.

Eleanor Marvin
National President

A Note of Thanks

The story of Justice for Children is an unfinished story. But even this installment is incomplete without expressing gratitude to the many people who contributed significantly to its development. From that long list, we would like to say a special thank you to:

The Children in Trouble Forum at the 1970 White House Conference on Children, particularly the young people there whose experience in life and the justice system presented an immediate challenge to act;

Milton Rector, Willis Thomas, Oliver J. Keller, Lois Forer, and Larry Cole, who believed in the value of citizen involvement and encouraged the initiation of the project;

and the police officers, lawyers, judges, probation officers and institutional staffs, to whom society has delivered its problems and whose cooperation made the study possible.

On their behalf, and on behalf of the National Council of Jewish Women, this book is dedicated to all our children—good, bad, and unlabeled—with whom we share Tomorrow.

Flora Rothman, Chairwoman
NCJW Justice for Children Task Force

Children
Without Justice

Introduction

O n December 14, 1970, when 4,000 delegates assembled in Washington, D.C. for the White House Conference on Children, some of the dozen representatives from the National Council of Jewish Women (NCJW) were obvious choices for one or other of the 24 different topics under study. Experience and volunteer activities, particularly in the field of day care, dictated their assignments. For other NCJW delegates, a computer helped out. In went delegate data, out came Conference assignment.

One such computer assignment turned out to be the first link in a chain of reactions and actions leading to the nationwide NCJW study-and-action program, Justice for Children. Within four years the program had moved from study to local action to national effort.

In the beginning, there was a routine computer match-up: Flora Rothman of Long Island, N.Y. to the Forum on Children in Trouble. The Forum chairman was Howard James, a Pulitzer Prize winner, who had reported and written extensively on the topic. From Monday through Thursday, the material unfolded: reports

1

from experts, statistical material, legal data, filmed material on institutions for the young, and a number of children to speak of their own experiences. Journalist James set the tone by speaking of children consigned to the "garbage can."

During four feverish days of meetings, when the NCJW delegates gathered informally each evening to compare notes, this Forum generated the most interest. Interest triggered concern and concern kindled determination to look further into the nationwide problem. After the conference, reactions became contagious as awareness of the problem moved from one level to another in NCJW. Similar reactions eventually emerged among individual members working on what became a national study involving about 3,000 Council members from 120 Sections (branches) in over 30 states.

The first practical step in the chronology of this effort was creation of the Justice for Children Task Force. It emerged from discussions involving Council's staff, president, national board, and national standing committees. The six-person Justice for Children Task Force was asked to immerse itself in the subject to determine how NCJW could become involved and what it could do.

The Task Force, made up of members from the New York metropolitan area, used their own state and local systems as testing grounds and observation places. With the assistance of experts they read, consulted, visited, observed, and "brainstormed" the topic. It was a learning process and sometimes a startling one as they came face to face with the system of juvenile justice.

"I found it very shocking to go through Juvenile Court for the first time," one Task Force member recalls. "Shocking to see the fear of authority in the children and in their families, shocking that in too many families children are a nuisance and the families want to get rid of them." On that first day in court, an official remarked that it was all a matter of "who got there first—whether a social worker cites a mother for neglect or the mother cites the child as troublesome because she wants, in effect, to get rid of the child." There was an initial reaction of anger, a feeling of outrage that children in trouble "were getting a raw deal from everybody they were involved with, from their parents on down."

Yet, as the Task Force soon realized, the system of juvenile justice was as large and as varied as the fifty states—sprawling, fragmented, localized, uplifted by bright spots, darkened by atrocities, all wrapped in a blanket of attitudes, assumptions, laws, procedures, bureaucratic habits, vested interests, good intentions, and disappointing results. The focus of the Task Force was not exposé, but self-education with the aim of identifying ways to improve the system. The search was not simply for what was wrong, but for what was going on, the good, the bad, and the uninterruptedly indifferent. The Task Force agreed on one overall point, thereby sharing the judgment of those who are part of the system of juvenile justice: major reforms are needed.

The next step was preparation of a manual, which would serve as "a guide to study and action." Published in April 1972, NCJW's *JUSTICE FOR CHILDREN* constituted an introduction to the subject with guidelines on how each Section could look into its own community situation. The manual made the key point that the system is so fragmented that each community presents "a distinctive portrait of strengths and flaws." It was a perfect match between the need for a national study of such a system and the nationwide structure of NCJW, with Sections located from coast to coast.

At about the same time, the subject of juvenile justice was presented in NCJW District Conventions. The prize-winning TV documentary of NBC News, *This Child Is Rated X* was used to introduce the various elements and individuals in the system of juvenile justice from children and parents to probation officers, judges, and directors of training schools. The documentary, which jolts viewers into awareness, was followed by panel discussions by experts.

This dual head-and-heart presentation elicited intense concern from the delegates, who were asked to share their reactions with their Sections at home. For them, as for members of the original Task Force, it was a hidden problem now starkly revealed. It cried out for action.

In the summer of 1972, when Eleanor Marvin, NCJW president, issued a call to all Sections to participate in local studies of the state of juvenile justice, her words reflected the strong feelings triggered by the subject. "It has been said that many captive animals in our country's zoos receive better treatment than some of the children imprisoned by American laws and society," she wrote. "How are the troubled and troublesome children of America handled? Wealthy parents who find their children hard to handle, send them away to school and camp in the summer; poor parents take them to juvenile court."

Individual Sections throughout the country responded by setting up introductory programs for their members along the same lines as the one presented in the District Conventions. After a showing of *This Child Is Rated X*, a panel of local experts discussed juvenile justice, with a Council member as moderator. It caught on. Taking the Task Force manual in hand, Council Sections plunged into the study phase by following the guidelines for examining each aspect of the system of juvenile justice.

Sections were cautioned to study before they leapt into action. In the course of examining the system, the temptation was strong to pursue piecemeal remedies as soon as need was identified. But this ran the risk of being shortsighted. In some cases, rather than help improve some facility, it might be wise to develop alternatives to the facility.

Reports started to come into national headquarters during the winter of 1972-73. By the spring of 1973, Lois Whitman of Council's national staff was able to report preliminary findings to the National Conference of Social Welfare. She reported that the Sections were amazed at the percentage of children who got into trouble just because of their age. They had done things that were crimes only for children: playing hooky, breaking curfews, running away from home, being "incorrigible." Among other things, she reported that Council members found that the "performance records of the institutions that were supposedly rehabilitating the children were terrible."

In line with Council's concern and commitment in the area of juvenile justice, NCJW's Hannah G. Solomon Award was presented in January 1973 to Lois G. Forer, a remarkable Philadelphia judge, who described her work as a lawyer for poor children facing the courts in a book titled, *No One Will Lissen.* The title was taken from the constant lament of 3,000 poor children represented between 1966 and 1968 by a special legal Office for Juveniles which she directed.

In accepting the award, Judge Forer spoke of children's rights and of the need to apply the benefits and protection of the U. S. Constitution to children. "Every child, like every adult, should have the right to liberty," she said. "Nobody should be locked up 'for his own good' unless he has committed a crime and forfeited his right to liberty—and then only after he has had a proper due process trial."

As Council members across the country became involved with the problems of juvenile justice, they were drawn increasingly to the newer concept of volunteering—volunteers as change agents in their communities. Rather than limit themselves to ameliorating symptoms, they were more and more involved in trying to cure the ailment. They presented testimony before governmental bodies and at official hearings. They were advocating as well as serving.

Recognition came in citations from such organizations as the National Conference of Social Welfare and the National Council of Juvenile Court Judges. Ongoing relationships were established by NCJW's national office with the Office of Youth Development of the U. S. Department of Health, Education, and Welfare; with the Justice Department's Law Enforcement Assistance Administration; and with the National Council on Crime and Delinquency. The manual prepared by the NCJW Task Force was distributed on request to universities, professional associations, and national organizations. The National Federation of Women's Clubs circulated the manual's "Community Score Card" to its chapters throughout the country for exploration of juvenile justice in their areas. Similar distribution was achieved by three follow-up handbooks with specific focal points: *Children's Rights, How to Set Up a Group Home*, and *Justice for Children Coalitions for Action.*

On the local level, recognition came to Sections and to their members. Individuals active in juvenile justice studies were appointed to city, county, and state units and commissions where they could influence policy. Local attention was exemplified in the fall of 1973 when the Greater Hartford (Conn.) Section received the twelfth annual G. Fox Award for the "Outstanding Performance of a Women's Community Organization." The award, presented at a luncheon which included the governor of Connecticut, came one year after the Greater Hartford Section launched its Justice for Children program. The award money was used to provide needed equipment for local detention and group homes.

While no two Sections proceeded in exactly the same way, Greater Hartford Section typified what was done from coast to coast by individual Sections working in their own communities. In teams of two or three women, the Greater Hartford Section Justice for Children Committee visited police departments, courts, detention homes, correctional institutions, schools, and social agencies. The Justice for Children manual was used, along with its guidelines, and the material recorded. As the result of this study phase, the Section:

1. Printed and distributed a 16-page summary of findings and recommendations.

2. Generated publicity to bring the situation to public attention.

3. Held two public meetings, which showed the documentary, *This Child Is Rated X*, followed by a panel-discussion by experts.

4. Testified at the Connecticut legislative hearings regarding runaways, residential facilities, and comprehensive services to children.

5. Enlisted interest and aid of other service organizations in establishing a state-wide coalition on Justice for Children.

6. Developed teams of volunteers to participate in service and research projects.

By the fall of 1974, more than eighty Sections had already begun the action phase of Justice for Children. They were at work to change legislation affecting children. They were involved in the establishment of group homes and drop-in centers; in volunteer services to children in court, on probation, and in institutions; and in mobilizing community action through public meetings and coalitions with other concerned groups.

Like news bulletins, reports came into the national headquarters of one action after another, a program here, an important appointment there, a new volunteer service or assistance for an old one, a campaign for new facilities or even, as in Louisville, Kentucky, a challenge to plans for a new one.

The Louisville example was instructive. It dramatized the importance of the study phase of the program. Instead of accepting the conventional wisdom that new and bigger is better, NCJW's Louisville Section and the Louisville Junior League (which collaborated on the study) questioned plans for a new jail-courts complex. A large juvenile detention center was designed as part of the complex, a plan that was challenged in a public campaign. Expert consultants were brought in; their publicized judgment was that the plan had "no redeeming features." The juvenile facility was judged to be in the wrong place at the wrong time for the wrong number (with three times as many beds as were needed).

The Louisville *Courier-Journal* came forward editorially on the side of the challenge. It declared that "fortunately for the community, a task force from the Louisville Section of the National Council of Jewish Women and the Louisville Junior League didn't wait for the public unveiling of the jail-courts complex before demanding the 'answering of all questions.'" The newspaper then labeled the answers as "lame." By the time the design for the jail-courts complex was formally presented, the juvenile detention facility was left out and further study called for. Then, in March, 1974, an official 15-member commission was named to study the city's entire system of juvenile justice and to make plans for upgrading it—with two past presidents of Louisville Section as commission members.

Over and beyond the public attention won by particular Council Sections in particular communities, there are the range, spread, and variety of actions by Council Sections. This can be suggested by examples from various parts of the country: tutoring at a detention home (Kansas City, Mo.); volunteers in court and at a guidance center (New Orleans, La.); working to set up a group home for runaway girls (Teaneck, N.J.); tutorial services and a job-development program at a counseling center (Portland, Ore.); campaign to amend the juvenile code, exploration of Big Sister projects (Pittsburgh, Pa.); home for runaway adolescents (Memphis, Tenn.); legislative and procedural recommendations to Juvenile Board (San Antonio, Tex.); organization of large-scale coalition (Tucson, Ariz.); volunteers in the probation department (Wilmington, Del.).

The report to the 1973 NCJW Convention reflected the emphasis on grass-roots involvement by noting that "the medals, plaudits, laurels, and bows must go to the Section chairwomen and their committees, and to the state coordinators." The report added: "These women took the handbook and used it with intelligence and imagination. They visited and interviewed critically and compassionately, and they were determined from the start that we would not 'just look' but would follow study with action."

The process had a powerful personal dimension for the women involved. It was called by many an "eye-opener," by others a first-hand experience that left no one untouched, and, throughout, it triggered strong feelings *to do something*. What at first was considered an interesting Council activity that attracted volunteers became a compelling involvement, mixing determination, feeling, and growing expertise. The women volunteers took their work seriously and were, in turn, taken seriously.

One example was unfolded to a member of the Justice for Children Task Force during a plane trip back from a national Council meeting. A fellow passenger described the efforts of her Section to improve juvenile facilities in their city. Section members went about town, knocking on doors, talking to local councilmen and city influentials, who listened politely but were not impressed enough to act. Then a child committed suicide in the local house of detention and the shock of it brought response. Suddenly, the city fathers started to pay attention and meaningful reforms were instituted. The volunteers bitterly regretted the fact that it took a child's suicide to produce action, but they also saw their efforts materialize in action.

The awareness of their efforts was brought home at a city gathering attended by the volunteer and her husband, a prominent lawyer in the city. The mayor singled out the couple at the reception and moved toward them with outstretched hand. The husband started to respond to the handshake until he realized that the mayor had come over to shake the wife's hand and say: "I really want to congratulate you and Council for what you have done in the town." It was the first time that her lawyer-husband realized the significance of his wife's volunteer work.

In committee after committee, in public hearings and in legislative debates—in city councils, state assemblies, and in Congress—the voice of NCJW was being heard as an expert advocate on behalf of children in trouble. But while working to dispel the general darkness surrounding children in trouble, NCJW was also lighting individual candles in local communities.

As the fourth anniversary of the 1970 White House Conference on Children approached, NCJW placed Justice for Children in a national context. The importance of a commitment by the federal government to setting of standards was being emphasized more than ever, as was the need for coordination of federal efforts. Over and above that, NCJW was looking to the society-wide problems that form a troubled and troublesome environment for the system of juvenile justice. It was no more than a reassertion of Council's historical interest in social problems, as noted by its president, Eleanor Marvin: "NCJW's efforts are not confined to the justice system. As our own studies have shown, health and educational needs and poverty are inextricably intertwined with problems of justice. Such problems have been our concern for over 80 years and will continue to be so as long as they, and NCJW, exist."

1 Enter the Child

Each year, about two million children are arrested. Over one million of these children become a matter of court record after getting into trouble with the law as it is variously applied to them in 2,800 jurisdictions. All of them are touched by a system of juvenile justice which penetrates every aspect of community life in America. The system involves more than police and probation officers, judges and other officials, administrators and institutional personnel; more than courts, detention centers and training schools. It reflects all of American society and represents a lien on the future, payable in the lives of the young.

This system intermittently arouses public concern, but usually operates outside public attention, a case of "benign neglect." For some 3,000 members of the National Council of Jewish Women who participated in the Justice for Children study, the system has become a matter of ongoing attention. They came up close to the system and it left impressions as varied as the nation's disparate, haphazard set of arrangements for children in trouble.

In the beginning and in the end, the NCJW observers were faced with the plight of children in the concrete, with what they saw and learned first-hand. Once
these flesh-and-blood encounters took place, indifference
was out of the question. The Council members were on
their way from feeling to learning to doing, from study
to action, a sequence that appropriately began with vivid
glimpses of the system of juvenile justice in its various
stages of operation.

In a courtroom, an attractive teenage girl was answering
a judge's questions in monosyllables. She had been in a
detention center for three months and this was her third
appearance, once each month to answer questions about
her father who was charged with raping her. Each
month, daughter and father were brought into court and
each time the policeman who had drawn up the
complaint did not appear. On the third court appearance,
the charge was dismissed, but since the girl could not
return home and since there was no other place to send
her at the time, she was sent back to the detention
center. A Council observer recalled the scene: "She had
that look of someone having absolutely no hope. Yet,
there were social workers in the courtroom and nothing
was being done for that girl. She was the victim. Her
father went free, but she was in custody. It was as
though she were the criminal, instead of being merely
the victim. She had done nothing—except that she was
under 18."

In Maryland, it was found that a 14-year-old boy was led
away from home in handcuffs by police after his parents
complained that he was out of control. Eventually, the
court investigated, found the parents needed intensive
psychiatric treatment, and placed the boy in a foster
home. The reason for the parents' complaint: the boy
would not take a bath.

Enter the Child

Outside a juvenile court, a member overheard a conversation between a boy coming from a detention center and his parents, as they awaited a hearing:

FATHER: I'll bet it feels funny being locked up, doesn't it? What was it like in there?

SON: You feel like an animal in a cage. It was awful.

FATHER: I didn't know it would be like that.

In Kansas, a co-chairwoman of a Justice for Children Committee described what a teacher told her, "not a very important story, but at the moment of its telling it said as much as any story I'd ever heard. In the school sector of the detention facility, the petite home economics teacher told of a young boy (held for murder) whom she had taught to prepare a few low-cost foods. With tears he had expressed his gratitude to her. His mother, he said, had deserted the family long before, and all they could afford or prepare had been beans. Now, he said, he knew he could do better for the family."

In a courtroom, a Council member watched a 15-year-old girl as her mother told the judge that the teenager "would be better off not returning to the community." When the mother added that the girl had not attended school, the girl said quietly to her mother: "You wouldn't let me." The girl's remark was ignored and she was returned to a detention center. As the teenager was being led from the courtroom, she turned at the door and cried out: "How long do I have to stay there?" No one answered.

A tour of a "showcase" training school included a scene in which a 13-year-old boy was introduced to the visitors by a staff person. "Show the ladies how we shine floors," the boy was told. Head bowed, the boy slipped a square of carpeting under one foot and began shuffling it back and forth. The boy's crime had been truancy.

As so many different experiences and observations blended with material gathered from coast to coast and as reports from more than one hundred Sections were assimilated at NCJW headquarters in New York, three themes emerged from this search for "Justice for Children:"

1. The system of juvenile justice was failing the young.

2. Improvements could be made, change was possible, outsiders could help.

3. Society in general and local communities in particular had to bear their responsibility.

The testimony of experts inside and outside the system coupled with the actual experiences and activities of Council Sections in their own communities corroborated the above conclusions. The more Justice for Children was examined the more it became apparent that each community must bear the responsibility for what happens to its children. It must face up to fundamental human needs of social as well as legal justice. Society gets the system of justice it wants or deserves.

The Chairman of the Senate Subcommittee to Investigate Juvenile Delinquency, Senator Birch Bayh of Indiana, summed up the failure in a speech before the Baltimore Section of NCJW: "No fancy phrases, nor colorful rhetoric can properly convey the extent to which the American system of juvenile justice has failed. It has failed the society that created it. And, more important, it has failed the very young it was supposed to help."

In testimony before Senator Bayh's subcommittee, NCJW cited the reports from its Sections that characterized local systems of juvenile justice as "confused, fragmented and disorganized," adding that "we are too often dealing with children's educational and family problems inappropriately in the judicial system."

As Council members delved into juvenile justice,

they were brought up short by the realities of one particular phenomenon: the "status offender." It referred to children who were in trouble only because they were children. The same acts would not bring adults into the clutches of the law. It was paradoxical in an American society which views itself as "child-centered."

Discriminatory and vague statutes characterize as offenses actions performed by those who have the status of children. A child can be brought to court for being "incorrigible" or "unruly" or "stubborn." Or a child's offense can be to "habitually idle away his or her time," play hooky or run away from home (even when home is hell). Non-criminal but rebellious acts, such as misbehaving in school, refusing to obey parents, staying out late and having "bad companions," can land a child in court. What Council members found bore out the harsh reality of what Howard James reported in investigating the juvenile justice system. He found thousands of children spending "months, even years, behind bars for offenses that would not put an adult in jail for an hour."*

Antiseptic acronyms hold a legal sword over children. They are called PINS, CHINS or CINS, MINS, and JINS—persons (children, minors or juveniles) in need of supervision. Or children in need of special supervision (NSS) or in need of adult supervision (NAS). Acronyms and labels aside, the meaning is clear. Children are arrested, become the subject of police and court records, and are sent away to institutions where they are kept under lock and key—all for behavior that is not criminal.

Of all children who get into trouble with the law, it has been estimated in federal surveys that "at least half of the delinquency referrals to the Juvenile Court are not offenses which would be considered crimes if committed by adults." On one visit to a state training school for boys 13 to 15 years of age, NCJW observers

---

*Howard James, *Children in Trouble* (New York: David McKay Co., Inc., 1969), p. 12.

were told that 85 percent were PINS. That meant only 15 percent had committed acts that are criminal for adults. Other estimates are not as high: the President's Task Force on Juvenile Delinquency and Youth Crime reported that about one out of four children appearing in juvenile courts, and the same proportion of those in state institutions for delinquent children, committed non-criminal acts. The category of "status offense," open to wide discretion, accounted for an especially high percentage of girls in institutions. In its 1971 report census of *Children in Custody*, the Justice Department found that 70 percent of girls detained or institutionalized were being held for "juvenile offenses," as compared to 23 percent of the boys.

Moreover, one state's definition is not another's. The age, criteria, procedures, and legal treatment of juveniles vary enormously. In some places, status offenders and delinquents from seven years of age can be put away in institutions; in others, from age 10. "Youthful offenders" can be youths over 14 who committed a felony; elsewhere, they can be anyone between 14 and 16 who gets into trouble with the law regardless of whether the act was a felony, a misdemeanor, or a status offense.

Other variations emerged when NCJW asked its state public affairs chairwomen to report on juvenile laws in their bailiwick. Status offenses had different descriptions in different states, making offenses an accident of geography. Moreover, statutes usually provided protection for the civil rights of adult offenders but seldom protected those of juvenile status offenders.

Differences appeared across the board in the 1972 survey. They were evident in the authority to detain minors, the circumstances under which detention is permitted and for how long, and the way juvenile courts and police records are handled. Instead of uniformity, there was bewildering and unjust or unjustified variety.

What emerged from all aspects of the NCJW study was a system with inherent flaws that confounded the many well-meaning people striving to make it work. The failure transcended the occasional examples of atrocities either by individuals or by particular facilities. More than children's rights before the law, children's place in society was at issue. A system whose intended goal was the good of children was working in the opposite direction.

In recent years, a much-publicized statement about this failure came from Milton Luger, speaking as president of the National Association of State Juvenile Delinquency Program Administrators and director of the New York State Division for Youth. In the course of describing the problems surrounding harassed administrators attempting to improve the system of rehabilitation, his words carried a portentous message that was echoed in findings of Council Sections: "With the exception of a relatively few youths, it is probably better for all concerned if young delinquents were not detected, apprehended, or institutionalized. Too many of them get worse in our care."

The president of the National Council on Crime and Delinquency, Milton Rector, made a similar assessment: "We probably would have less crime if fewer criminals were caught and sent to jail. The boys who aren't caught succeed far better in avoiding a life of crime than those who are caught and brought into the criminal justice system."

Paradoxes and conflicts abounded when the NCJW Task Force and Sections delved into the system of juvenile justice. They came to the surface from the sea of details in individual reports and they prompted observations such as these:

Children who get into trouble frequently have not learned the acceptable modes of rebellion and of withdrawal. When they "act out," they get into trouble.

When middle-class children get into trouble, justice tends to wear blindfolds. The disadvantaged, the poor, the minorities lack the know-how, the family backup and the resources to escape a system which operates with wide discretionary powers.

Children can get into trouble as they seek identity and if they become enmeshed in the system, they become involved in a process that deprives them of privacy and destroys identity.

When the system defines a child as deviant, that's what he or she is likely to become. It is a harsh rule of self-fulfilling expectation.

When interviewed, the professionals in the system did not have their eyes closed. They were painfully aware of what was wrong. As one NCJW report noted: "In this state, we have people who are running a rehabilitation system whose very existence is of questionable value, even to themselves." With the exception of some professionals who did not want "outsiders to butt in," the majority realized that hope for progress rested on opening the windows. They were eager to have citizens understand what was going on and to arouse their interest. They made it clear that the system of juvenile justice depends on laws and budgets, on public attitudes and public support.

Nor was it a new struggle, as an 83-year-old Council member reminded a Louisville meeting. In the 1930's she had worked for reform of juvenile justice. "I admit, with humility, we didn't stick to the fight," she said. "You are fighting deep-rooted prejudice against 'naughty' children. If you really can stay with it, it's a fight worth fighting."

As NCJW members learned as soon as they came into contract with the system, proximity breeds awareness. Walking into a waiting area of a juvenile court, seeing a detention center for children, talking to teenagers in a training school, listening to an administrator describe what he or she faces—all these experi-

ences provided what was described as "instant education." They shattered euphemisms that abound in the
system of juvenile justice: youth centers (locked detention facilities), uniformed court officers (bailiffs), law
guardians (lawyers for children), youth counselors and
child care workers (prison guards). Training schools are
presented as places with "rolling campuses" where children live in "cottages," not as one youth worker realistically labelled them—"junior jails."

"There is no substitute for walking into a place
and getting the feel of it," one Task Force member
pointed out. "A set of blueprints or plans wouldn't tell
you a thing. It doesn't tell you whether it's a cold, harsh
place; it doesn't tell you whether the kids are sitting
around, as one woman reported, 'in limbo.' You can't get
the feeling of what happens in Juvenile Court without
sitting in the court and watching cases come up and
seeing the kids and seeing the parents and seeing the
interaction between the judge and other people in the
courtroom. You can read a court transcript or an official
report, but that is only a skeleton."

It was not so much that the women observers
saw atrocity and brutality from one end of the system to
the other. It was much less tangible. They came back not
with tales full of horror but of stalemate. NCJW members who had seen the atrocities in the TV documentary,
This Child Is Rated X, and who had read about abuses
often had a strange reaction. It was not as bad as expected; it just wasn't good.

"When you first go to visit institutions, you
really don't see very brutalizing things," one woman recalled. "At first, you think it's not too bad, but then you
start thinking of the things you really saw and you real-
ize that you really hadn't seen anything. You didn't see
anything being done *to* the children. But, also, you didn't
see very much being done *for* them."

Council members responded to their experiences
in two directions. One, they worked to improve the op-

eration of the system by providing volunteer services and by organizing projects affiliated with the system. Two, they committed themselves to bring about changes in facilities, procedures, and laws. The study phase of Justice for Children had enabled them to identify places where input was needed and would provide significant benefits. As they became well-versed, they were tapped for memberships on boards and commissions concerned with children. When the time came, they were prepared to speak with authority built on knowledge they had acquired. They had not gone from armchair to witness chair, but from watching and studying the system up close to first-hand testimony.

One result was a variety of appointments where Council members have a voice in making policy and in making changes. Typically, members have been named to a newly-formed Youth Assistance Commission Authority (Louisiana), to an advisory group of the State Crime Commission (Georgia), to a committee on privacy and security of police and court records (Oregon), to the Governor's Commission for Children and Youth (Maryland), to the Boards of Youth Service Bureaus (New York, Florida and Tennessee), to the Citizen's Committee for Family Court (New York), and to the chairman of the Kentucky Commission for Children and Youth. In Pennsylvania, after a Council member was asked to help chair an inspection team to visit a detention center, the resulting report helped close the facility.

Evidence began to accumulate of the Justice for Children program's impact on local communities. Most significantly, it had begun to raise public consciousness of the subject as newspapers throughout the country reported on NCJW forums and findings. As one Maryland newspaper noted, in an article describing improvements in the state's juvenile services, "Much of the current interest in juveniles could stem from the Annapolis branch of the National Council of Jewish Women."

Other organizations joined in local Justice for

Enter the Child

Children coalitions, including legal and labor organizations, social action and religious groups, and representatives from state and local governments and governmental departments. Coalitions took on issues, such as the removal of status offenders from court jurisdiction, and projects, like community education, juvenile court monitoring and the establishment of group homes.

Beyond the problems inside the system of juvenile justice, there was the society outside. The problems are far greater than the system alone can handle. The most basic solutions lie outside it. This was the third theme that emerged after the NCJW was aroused by failure in the system to work on changes and improvements: it was necessary to look to society's responsibility.

The juvenile justice system has become a dumping ground for society's problems. The overburdened court, which should be a place of last resort, gives testimony to a society-wide pattern of evasion and even irresponsibility. Such a harsh view became inescapable as the reports began to form a national pattern.

A mismatch existed. An assortment of social, educational, psychological, and family problems were being shunted into a system for handling quasi-criminal matters, a system whose operations paralleled criminal procedures for adults. The system of juvenile justice just could not solve the set of problems handed over by local communities. Those inside the system have been trying to put this situation in perspective, including distinguished jurists like Chief Judge David J. Bazelon of the U. S. District Court of Appeals, Washington, D. C. Writing for those in the system, he stated in the *Juvenile Court Journal:*

The battle against juvenile crime can't possibly be won in court, even in the most enlightened court. That is only where we bring the worst casualties and hope that some, with good care, will survive, albeit with scars and crippling disabilities. The name of the game is

Prevention, and that's a job for the institutions in the community that can help children without stigmatizing them, without labeling them delinquents and saddling them with a court record for the rest of their lives. The institutions that can handle that job may not exist. But it's up to you to call attention to the need, and not to go on pretending you can do the job yourselves.

A special report to the Appellate Divisions of New York's First and Second Departments made a similar point in March 1973 in describing the impossible task handed to the system of juvenile justice:

The Family Court has, in effect, become the place to which children who may be delinquent or persons in need of supervision are brought only because they are beset with emotional, psychological, and social problems which are rooted in poverty, deplorable housing and a destructive home environment. The Family Court is resorted to because society has not addressed itself to the causes of the child's internal turmoil, nor provided community resources that would offer the necessary remedial services.

The large number of reports prepared by individual NCJW Sections documented the validity of such observations. As a Connecticut NCJW observer noted, "The Court lacks sufficient resources to handle a variety of problems in a variety of ways—it almost seems to say to a troubled youngster, 'Come back and see us when you're in greater trouble . . . maybe we can help you then.' "

In one community after another, the needs of children were not being met and the conditions which victimized them were not being remedied. Two strands usually ran parallel in local communities: ignorance of the problem and indifference to it. Communities did not know what was the matter, and they were not paying attention in the first place. As one NCJW committee in Michigan reported, "In our state, people of good will are fighting the windmills of indifference, lack of funds, stereotyping, poor housing, clothing, and education. These things will be much harder to overcome than the concrete things such as a child being placed in detention without the order of a judge."

Poor, disadvantaged and minority children suffer the most from the failure of their communities. It has been estimated that a black youth living in a city has a 90-percent chance of being arrested because color and class play such an important part in whether a youngster gets arrested. (In one survey, 9 out of 10 college students admitted that as children, they had committed at least one act for which they could have been—but were *not*—arrested.) A New York Section noted that a large percentage of the children they saw were black and Puerto Rican: "Their lives reflected the problems of poverty, illiteracy, unemployment, and drugs. With no positive image and little hope of success, children commit crimes or are neglected or abused or are uncontrollable or mentally ill."

After going out into the field as well as examining numerous Section reports, one member of the Justice for Children Task Force remarked: "My impression of the whole juvenile system was that it was inequitable. Children from well-to-do or middle-class homes very seldom see the inside of a court; they are usually able to bypass the entire system. On the other hand, minority and disadvantaged children whose families lack resources, and who live in areas where police are inclined to assume they get into trouble, go through the whole thing." Whether rich or poor, white or black, many children were seen as being short-changed by a juvenile justice system ill-fitted to confront their basic needs. "It is a very degrading system, which can change a child who may have done a very minor thing into a hardened criminal."

Seventy-five years after the first juvenile court in the United States was established in Illinois in 1899, such a view of the system was ironic. The system had begun with idealism when reformers succeeded in establishing special courts for children to separate them from hardened adult criminals. Special courts would provide special treatment of children in trouble. They operated under the rational of *parens patriae,* of the judge as substitute parent, with primary concern not for crime and punishment but for the best interests of the child. By 1925, all but two states had established special courts for children; currently there is a juvenile court in every jurisdiction, with some 2,800 courts hearing children's cases. By the time of the NCJW study, the optimism of 75 years ago had changed to concern about the enormous discretionary powers of the courts and about decisions affecting a child's entire life that could be made in three to five minutes by a busy judge. A system created to protect children was not only failing in this mandate; it was operating to their detriment.

Serious questions faced NCJW Sections as they examined not one nationwide system of juvenile justice, but a multitude of diverse local systems. On one hand, juvenile justice defied generalizations; on the other, patterns of failures were repeated everywhere. In each aspect of the system, from intake to probation, from detention to institutionalization, similar shortcomings were evident. At the same time, meaningful reforms, changes, and activities were located, with potential applications to other places and other communities. In-depth examination and description of this nationwide study will, in the ensuing chapters, cover these various aspects, linking what was learned to what was done. Among the crucial issues:

What "offenses" bring children into the juvenile justice system? Are they valid?

Does discretion foster unequal treatment?

Enter the Child

What are the legal rights of children? How should they be safeguarded?

How are juvenile records used and abused?

Are personnel properly selected and trained—from policemen to judges, from administrators and probation officers to guards and supervisors?

Why are children in institutions? Can these institutions meet their needs? What are the alternatives?

As citizens, what is our responsibility?

Such questions were raised, examined, documented and discussed in Section reports. Channeled through the NCJW Task Force, they provide a multi-faceted view of justice for children.

Step by step, the system of juvenile justice operates inexorably, beginning with that crucial first step when a child encounters the law.

2 The Gatekeepers

Each time a child comes into contact with the law, a community goes on trial for its system of justice for children. Procedures, regulations and laws reflect the community's priorities and attitudes. The gatekeepers for the system—police and intake officers—lead the child into a network in which neighborhood, school, family and court make decisions with broad discretionary power.

Each time a child comes into contact with the law, the community pays not only the bill, it pays the social price when it fails to deal effectively with children in trouble. But the child stands to pay the highest price of all. He or she could be at a turning point toward a scarred life, or worse, toward a life of crime.

At the initial encounter between the child and the system of juvenile justice, police and court-intake officials play their crucial roles as gatekeepers. Generally, they try to keep the young out of the system for the children's own sake. This constructive approach was evident from coast to coast in the NCJW study, allowing for those communities where a "law and order" attitude prompts policemen to pull children in. Many children who are not diverted initially from the justice system by the police are diverted by the intake unit of the courts.

Due to diversionary practices by police and intake officers, only one-eighth of the youngsters who come into contact with the law are handled through judicial action. Robert J. Gemignani, former Commissioner of the U. S. Youth Development and Delinquency Prevention Administration, indicated the proportion of children diverted at each stage:

It is estimated, conservatively, that almost 4,000,000 youth had police contact in 1970 and that 2,000,000 of those contacts resulted in arrests, half of which were referred to juvenile courts. Of the million referred to juvenile courts, about half were counselled and released with no further action; the other half were handled officially through some form of court hearing.

As primary gatekeepers for the system, the police are called upon to reverse their traditional role of working to put offenders behind bars. The courtroom is, properly speaking, the last resort for concerned police officials, particularly those specializing as juvenile officers. In dealing with juvenile offenses, the increasingly enlightened police view is that the problems are primarily social rather than criminal and that the best interests of society are served by diverting youngsters from the justice system.

When approached by NCJW members, police departments were cooperative, presenting a self-image along these lines:

We (the police) are doing the best job possible under the circumstances. The main problems in juvenile justice lie outside the police departments; they reside in the parents, the schools, the community, the society-at-large. More often than not, we are involved where we should not be involved as police officials simply because the community is not taking care of its problems. So children in trouble land in the lap of the police.

This self-image is illustrated in outspoken attitudes of juvenile police officials in NCJW reports from all parts of the country. On parents: "biggest problem in this work is the need for better understanding between parent and child" (East); "parents are probably one of the greatest problems we have" (Southwest); "lack of guidance, discipline and concern on the part of parents" (East); "many parents tend to overprotect children and not encourage them to be responsible individuals; there are also parents who deny the seriousness of the problem" (Midwest). On the community: "Whatever is being done isn't working. The news media, our permissive society, lack of vocational training and inadequate recreational facilities all contribute to the juvenile program. . . . The police could cooperate with other civic organizations, but the public is apathetic. We need communication and cooperation" (East).

Repeatedly, police officials stressed what one Illinois official called a double standard of justice for children, one for the city and one for the suburbs: "Police in the suburbs seem to be more understanding and more lenient." A Wisconsin official described the "world of difference" between central city and suburb. In the suburbs, children are not taken into custody, but are turned over to their parents; a policeman who does not follow this procedure "usually doesn't last very long on the police force." In the inner city, the policeman takes children into custody for such things as loitering and truancy; "the more children he apprehends the more he is respected by the other policemen." In a Massachusetts suburb, the policeman was described as a "father figure" ready to overlook many minor incidents that "would be guaranteed to land in trouble" disadvantaged children in the nearby city.

The Gatekeepers

In the NCJW reports, the difference between city and suburban police reflects the disadvantage of being non-white and poor. It increases the likelihood of getting picked up by the police. Recently published research covering boys in Philadelphia 10 to 18 years of age bore out the point. Whereas one out of three white boys ended up on police records, one out of two non-white boys did. On the same offense, a non-white had a greater chance of being arrested. Only 48 percent of white boys who committed serious offenses were arrested, compared with 68 percent of non-white boys. When the boys were compared according to socioeconomic status, about one-fourth were delinquent (26.5 percent) in the higher class, compared with almost one-half (44.8 percent) in the lower status.*

What stands out is the discretionary power of the policeman wherever and whenever he encounters a child. Such laws as those governing curfews or loitering are particularly susceptible to arbitrary enforcement.

Police exercise discretionary power at two points in the encounter with juveniles—on the street and after bringing them in for what is called a "stationhouse adjustment" of reprimand and release. The offense and the evidence aside, the child's attitude can tilt the scales between arrest and no-arrest, between filing a complaint with the court and keeping the youth out of court. In two New Jersey counties, for instance, the form for referring children to court allowed for the usual information on name, address, offense, etc.; the final item was "Attitude," with a place to check "Respectful" or "Disrespectful." "If a child has a foul mouth and he can be talked to, we will send him home," remarked one policeman. "On the other hand, if he persists, it is a sign of open defiance. I would bring him to the station and sit him down and talk to him on a one-to-one basis."

*This study by three University of Pennsylvania criminologists, Marvin E. Wolfgang, Robert M. Figlio, and Thorsen Sellin, was described in *Delinquency in a Birth Cohort* (University of Chicago Press, 1973).

Two researchers illustrated the importance of attitude by examining the way a random sample of police officers would make a decision to arrest a juvenile. The policemen were selected from three departments in a northeastern metropolitan area and presented with a typical case: a 14-year-old boy picked up for being drunk and disorderly in public. They were handed 24 pieces of information for making a decision and, as it turned out, the most critical consideration for reaching a final decision was "attitude of offender." This factor triggered the arrest decision in 75 percent of the officers studied. In no instance did the policemen regard the offense alone as enough of a basis to make a decision. In the case at hand, the youth was described as "belligerent," questioning the officer's authority to take him into custody. Fifteen of the officers decided at this point to arrest him, with three deciding to release him with a warning.*

Another study has found that "defiance on the part of a boy will lead to an appearance in juvenile court quicker than anything else." The "right" attitude clearly works in a child's favor, as has been recommended by the National Advisory Commission on Criminal Justice Standards and Goals. The Commission recommended that attitude not be a factor in deciding whether to arrest adults, but that it be considered in work with children: "With juvenile offenders, attitude may properly be weighed in deciding whether to divert youths from the juvenile justice system."* NCJW reports indicate that while a "positive" attitude may lead to a youngster's diversion from the juvenile justice system, a "negative" attitude, which may be fear or defensiveness interpreted as arrogance or disrespect, may lead a youngster into the system.

A use of discretion is illustrated in an actual case involving a 14-year-old identified as one of a group of boys who had broken lights outside an ice cream parlor by throwing snowballs. The boy was known to the po-

*Dennis C. Sullivan and Larry J. Siegel, "How Police Use Information to Make Decisions," *Crime and Delinquency*, July 1972, p. 261.

The Gatekeepers

lice juvenile bureau in a suburban area of New York, which had four cards in his file: reported missing by his father; found swimming without permission in a private pool; found in possession of a stolen bike; on probation for arson. His mother said he lied when caught in the act and that a psychiatrist had been unable to communicate with him. A detective who had worked on the boy's arson case advised: "You have nothing to gain by locking this kid up. He's gone that route. I think the kid should go out and get a job to pay for it." Soon after, the boy came in with his father, admitted he had broken at least one light and agreed to pay for the damage. The next day, he phoned again to report that the other boys had agreed to do the same. Acting as gatekeepers, the police had kept the case out of the juvenile justice system. One wonders, if this child had been the poor, black resident of an urban ghetto, would he instead be on his way to a career in and out of courts and training institutions.

Attitude works on both sides. Police with a "get-tough" approach are more likely to arrest youngsters. Some NCJW reports suggest that these officers take their cues from police higher-ups, who in turn are cued by city officials, who in turn are tuned to public attitudes. Where such an approach was evident in a West Coast city, youngsters in trouble responded with harsh descriptions of the police, as did one girl in a residential treatment center:

From my own experience personally, I wouldn't call a policeman even if I were dying. They would even give dope to kids. So many cops couldn't care less what happens to kids. They aren't even doing their duty anymore. Too many of them don't care. . . . If they know you have a record, anything you do, you'll be taken in. Once they picked up another girl as a runaway and picked me up, too, as I answered this description of a runaway. The cop said when I was released, 'If I ever see you again, I'll bust you.'

This get-tough attitude was also noted by a probation worker in the same metropolitan area, who remarked that the police "know who the 'bad' kids are and are constantly after them."

In communicating with a youngster, even the most benevolent policeman often must overcome the cold, intimidating atmosphere of the stationhouse. It takes little imagination to sense the impact upon a child in trouble brought in by a policeman. As one NCJW observer noted, "For even the casual visitor, entrance into Police Headquarters, with its tiled walls, cold linoleum or marble flooring, the straight-backed chairs and stark wooden desks, is a forbidding experience. One wants to get one's business done as quickly as possible and one prefers not to think of having to spend many hours there, especially being detained by the police."

In some communities, the police felt that the courts were letting juveniles "back on the streets too quickly," that judges were demonstrating too much "flexibility" and that tougher laws should be enacted. Possibly the epitome of such an attitude was the police captain running a juvenile division in a New England city. He urged putting away youthful offenders to protect the community and projected an attitude which drew criticism from social service professionals about his non-cooperation with youth programs aimed at prevention. The police captain was outspoken in citing the biggest weakness of the courts as losing control over a juvenile who has been committed to the youth services unit. Reflecting traditional police concern that those who commit a serious crime would be free to do it again, he said, "Many youngsters have been remanded to the Department of Youth Services and have been released in one or two days, even when they were guilty of assault and battery with a dangerous weapon, unarmed robbery and auto theft." He wanted juveniles accused of serious offenses to be tried in the regular criminal court because "we have to do this to get kids into jail."

The Gatekeepers

Two-thirds of the police departments visited in the NCJW studies reported that they have written guidelines to protect against misuse of discretionary police power. But even with guidelines, their application depends on the attitudes of higher-ups as well as the policeman on the street. In one West Coast metropolitan area, a policeman commented that the guidelines and orders "are being changed all the time so that many officers feel they can use their own discretion in booking a child." Other police noted that "there are no hard and fast guidelines used for taking a child into custody," and that "Family Court could not handle the caseload if every kid picked up were sent to court."

The intent of the guidelines is to prescribe criteria that will ensure even-handed treatment of children facing arrest and detention, and protection of their legal rights. Guidelines in one Texas city require that a juvenile's family or guardian be notified "without delay" when a child is taken into custody; in a New Jersey version, the police were ordered to make "immediate arrangements" to release juveniles to the custody of a parent or "suitable adult." As much as possible, guidelines call for release of juveniles to appropriate custody whenever possible, and for proper procedures. "Every care must be exercised to assure the rights of the child; he is guaranteed the same right as an adult," the Texas guidelines state.

Superseding the necessity for police guidelines for release versus detention is the issue of who should have authority to make the decision to place a child in detention. NCJW supports the National Advisory Commission on Criminal Justice Standards and Goals, which states:

"The detention decision should not be made by law enforcement officers, whose professional backgrounds and missions may differ considerably from those of court or social service personnel."

With or without guidelines, the NCJW study found police aware of the legal rights of children facing criminal charges, undoubtedly reflecting the impact of court decisions along these lines. However, practice varied from one community to another, even in adjacent suburban communities. In one Illinois suburb the child is informed of his legal rights, when taken into custody; in the suburb next door, he is not. Awareness of children's legal rights was not consistently translated into proper protection of such rights. There was a disturbing gap between rights on paper and rights in practice, a gap that varied not only by community and police department, but even by the individual police officer. Court decisions on the rights of children, including the right to legal counsel, will be discussed in a later chapter.

In one New Jersey community, a child is informed of his rights when the police official feels it might become a court case, a decision that may not be made until two or three days later. Meanwhile, the child has spoken to the police about his offense. Under a recent ruling, police officers in a major Florida city were prohibited from discussing the reasons for arrest with a child unless an attorney was present. However, it turned out that most parents encouraged their child to talk to the police officer about what happened, regardless of whether or not the required attorney was present.

On the other hand, in an upstate New York town, a child's rights are explained in front of his parents, and the policeman leaves the room if a child starts to discuss the case without parents or attorney present. In Connecticut, the child, parents, and attorney are advised of the child's rights, including the right to be silent. In a New York suburb, a policeman brings a child to a juvenile room at the stationhouse where a detective tells the child his rights, questions him and writes a report. After this is done, the parents are contacted and the child, along with his parents, is once again told of his rights.

The Gatekeepers

In one Texas city, detention is limited to criminal acts only, and parents no longer can request detention for their children. Children involved in misdemeanors are given citations and released. The next day they report to the detention center for discussion of the case with juvenile officials. This is in keeping with the firm recommendation made in a *Juvenile Court Journal* article that "most police units need constant reminders of the purpose of detention and their role in screening out those not needing secure or protective custody."

Many Sections incorporated recommendations into their findings, such as:

Police departments require special juvenile divisions. These should be adequately staffed on a 24-hour basis and should offer police officers status commensurate with the rest of the department.

Police departments would benefit from the use of counselors to work with runaways and truants.

Police need more information about community resources, particularly in light of the diversionary role played by the police.

Youth officers need specialized and in-service training to improve their understanding of juveniles and minority groups.

The last recommendation was stressed by the large majority of Section reports on their communities. Police awareness of this need was summed up by one police official in New Jersey: "The police officer should be educated in the areas of juvenile behavior so that he may best know how to recognize *causes of the conduct exhibited by the individual.* This should not be construed to justify the offense committed by the youngster, but so that we may better understand how to deal with the best interests of children." (Emphasis at police officer's request.)

The training which is provided youth officers is an indication of how committed the police department and the community are to effective handling of juveniles. Opposites could be found close to each other, as in two adjacent Midwest cities, where one sends its youth officers to a university for special training, and the other provides no training. Of some 60 police departments on which such information was obtained, about half reported that youth officers received special training. One-fourth reported some training and the other one-fourth, none. For the most part, special training appeared to come after, rather than before, assignment. Taking one Midwestern state as an example, 56 percent of its police departments do not require any training before assigning officers to juvenile work. Only 20 percent require prior training. In some areas, officers are selected for juvenile work because of their youth and interest in the young; sometimes because as family men they are more likely to be understanding. Outside metropolitan areas, in particular, selection criteria are likely to depend on the attitude of the police chief.

Across the board, the nature, quantity, and quality of training for juvenile work leaves much to be desired. Nor can this training be realistically limited to officers specializing in juvenile cases, since all policemen have considerable contact with young people in trouble. (In a Tennessee city, it was estimated that 70 percent of all police work involved juveniles.) Typically, juvenile matters get short shrift in police training programs, though there are exceptions. The Los Angeles Police Department, which is particularly concerned about youth programs, includes 12 hours on juvenile work in the general police training program of 19 weeks. Indications are that even this limited amount is more than most police departments provide.

Reports show police taking advantage of a variety of training opportunities in the area of juvenile problems. Minnesota has a Juvenile Officers Institute at

The Gatekeepers

the University of Minnesota where six-to-eight weeks of summer training are provided in such areas as problems of adolescence, methods of handling and counseling juveniles, and use of community agencies. Los Angeles sends two members of each police training class to attend a three-month course at the University of Southern California's Delinquency Control Institute. In-service training programs were also reported in some police departments, but these were limited in number. In addition, juvenile officers are encouraged, though not required, to take courses on their own at local colleges or at special institutes.

The type of commitment that makes an effective juvenile officer is typified by a Pasadena, Calif. policeman who received newspaper attention for his part in a One-Plus-One project aimed at 12-to-14-year-olds. An Army paratroop veteran, 33-year-old Patrolman Robert Graham works the midnight shift and during the day goes to a college specializing in training teachers for pre-schoolers. He decided to attend that particular college because: "If you're going to learn about adults or teenagers, go to the little kids to learn what makes them tick. The problems of kids are carried right over to adulthood." The One-Plus-One project uses a counseling team of an adult plus a youngster a little older than a child just starting to get into trouble for such actions as running away or stealing a bicycle. The project tries to reach the youngster as early as possible, Patrolman Graham notes, in order to cope with the feeling of youngsters rich and poor who "don't think they're worth a nickel . . . Basically, we try to teach all these kids how to cope with life. We try to teach kids some self-worth."

In various police departments, breakthroughs have been made in creating effective juvenile operations and in improving the police image with youngsters. One New Jersey police department has hired two social workers for its juvenile bureau, while in another county a lieutenant keeps track of truants and finds jobs for dropouts. A New York City precinct opened a storefront community relations center so that neighborhood people could come in to discuss their problems. On Long Island, youth officers hold rap sessions with young people, speak at the local schools, sponsor youth groups and, in the summer, the county hires 25 youngsters as aides. Several Sections reported local Officer Friendly programs, such as the one in Atlanta which offers, in addition to talks in schools, dances and other recreational activities. In California a police department experiment has delinquent boys accompany officers on their tours of duty.

Overall, many police departments are inadequately organized to deal with juvenile cases. One-fourth of the reports noted that no special juvenile divisions existed in the police departments. This is undoubtedly a more favorable figure than would be the case if it included more rural areas. In this instance, as in others throughout the NCJW study, the information reflects the location of NCJW Sections in areas with substantial Jewish populations. These tend to be large cities and suburbs of cities where facilities and resources are likely to be better than in smaller towns and rural areas.

Moreover, where a juvenile division existed, it was commonly undermanned as well as undertrained. Such police units handle a growing volume of juvenile cases, involving apprehension and investigation, interviewing children and parents, drawing up reports, offering testimony, and, in some cases, making referrals and aiding in the disposition of cases. The problem of inadequate staff is highlighted when the ratio of police juvenile officers to juveniles handled per year is compared. The ratio in NCJW reports varies from 1 to 42 (eastern suburb) to 1 to 600 (eastern city).

Even if youngsters go no further in their contact with the law than the stationhouse, they can acquire a police record. In some cases, an encounter between a child and a policeman on the beat is enough; it is noted on a card and filed. Theoretically, police records on juveniles are temporary and confidential; in practice, they are maintained indefinitely in many police departments. The survival of such records, sometimes under a different name, was evident in Section reports: records "are kept indefinitely—first in a 'juvenile file,' then in an 'overage' file" (city in Texas); "Files are destroyed on discretion of the Juvenile Division" (New Jersey town); "Law forbids keeping records of juveniles detained or arrested; but Youth Bureau keeps an 'information file,' separate from Police Department files. This file is never destroyed" (Connecticut city); "Offenders may request sealing of their records after five years; however, the records as such can never be erased" (metropolitan area in California); "It was hard to pinpoint for what offenses children are taken into custody, but one impression was that they were brought in for everything and a record was made. Then they were released to their parents or others" (Illinois suburb); "Technically, a juvenile's offenses are expunged when he reaches the age of 18. But the provisions for expunging records are not uniformly followed, since records dating back to 1938 are still available in our community" (upstate New York); "Records are kept forever" (Illinois suburb).

By the admission of various police departments, their records on juveniles remain incomplete—to the detriment of the youngsters. When charges are dropped or dismissed or youths found not guilty, police records are not necessarily brought up to date. The unfair and inaccurate stain remains, usually because of inadequate liaison between police and court, lack of clerical manpower or faulty and lax procedures. While various forms of confidentiality are maintained on such files, police departments vary in handling records, with government agencies having access to them. The NCJW Task Force was particularly concerned about a nationwide tendency to imperil confidentiality, particularly with the use of computers to centralize police records under the aegis of the U.S. Justice Department. As a result, the Task Force took a strong policy stand on the use and misuse of police juvenile records, stressing the key points that they be confidential and expungeable. The details of this stand will be discussed in the final chapter.

As the process of juvenile justice unfolds, a secondary gatekeeper comes to the forefront: the court official handling intake, usually an experienced probation officer. While police are the major source of referrals to court intake, other sources are departments of social services, schools, and parents or relatives. Police referrals include village, city, county, and state police; also railroad police and other types of special police officials.

Parents may refer their children to probation intake as a way of threatening them, something that schools are also tempted to do. As one probation officer noted, there is "a growing dependency of the public schools on the police and courts to control their student bodies, particularly in urban areas." Other parents in poverty areas resort to the courts as a way of getting social services for children who are in need rather than in trouble. In a joint statement, representatives of social service agencies in Connecticut underlined the "sad fact" that many children who need social services "must actually be arrested before any attempt is made to deal with their needs."

While 60 percent represents a typical proportion of juveniles who are diverted from the court system at intake, the proportion was as high as 80 percent in the reports from some NCJW Sections. The alternatives to referral to the court process are dismissal (sometimes with a warning), placing the youngsters on nonjudicial supervision, or referring the youngster to an agency which can provide helpful services.

Discretion is extensive, particularly with regard to status offenses that apply uniquely to children and have a wide interpretation by their very nature. A typical state code lists violations of laws or ordinances and then, in a second category, the following as the basis for swearing out a complaint against a child:

Habitual vagrancy

Incorrigibility

Immorality

Knowingly associating with thieves or vicious or immoral persons

Growing up in idleness or delinquency

Knowingly visiting gambling places or patronizing other places or establishments, his admission to which constitutes a violation of law

Habitual truancy from school

Deportment endangering the morals, health, or general welfare of the child.

The procedure in one New England city, as described in a Section report, typifies what happens when a youngster faces a delinquency charge. After a complaint is drawn up, the child is called in by a written notice, to be accompanied by parent or guardian. They are advised of the right to remain silent and to have a lawyer, along with the court's obligation to provide a lawyer if they cannot afford one. They then are asked to sign a waiver that they have been so informed. The child is then asked if he is guilty as accused and if he admits guilt, he must sign a statement of responsibility. At this point, the probation officer conducts a social investigation on the youngster which takes from one to three months. If the youngster denies guilt, the case is sent to an advocate (the court's lawyer) to decide whether there is enough evidence to bring the case to court. Certain offenses must go to court, with others handled entirely by the probation officer. In this particular city, the probation officers handle three-fourths of the cases entirely. One-fourth continue on through the judicial process.

Judging from Section reports, most Probation Departments have formal guidelines on intake procedures. Of those responding to questions in this area, seventy percent had guidelines, twenty-four percent did not, and six percent of the probation departments did not handle intake. Besides calling for release of juveniles to the custody of their parents or guardians, guidelines underscore the rights of children. But, once again, discretion predominates in practice.

In some cities, the probation officer informally "carries" youngsters on his roster, placing the legal process in limbo. This is regarded as a "straightening out" period, during which youngsters are, in effect, given a chance to mend their ways and are warned of court action otherwise. In a few cases substantial social services are offered to children and parents during this period. Often the child is merely called upon to demonstrate good behavior, and only in the case of bad behavior will he receive additional help.

When youngsters have nowhere to go—at home or in the community—and if the gatekeepers bring them through the doorway to the court system without diverting them, they enter into a form of punishment that is called detention.

3 Detention as Punishment

Generally speaking, when detention is properly used, the children in detention will be among the community's most disturbed and aggressively acting-out adolescents . . . Their detention experience cannot be a neutral one. It will either be a destructive experience confirming them in a pattern of delinquent behavior, or a constructive one that will help redirect them into becoming socially useful citizens. The mission of detention is to provide a constructive experience.*

These principles provide a point of departure for NCJW Sections visiting detention centers in their own communities to observe them firsthand. Detention facilities, operating as way stations between the police and the courts, are designed to provide temporary care for children who require "secure custody." The care was of varying kinds, the custody was a matter of lock and key, the "constructive experience" was more the exception than the rule. Repeatedly detention emerged as a form of punishment without conviction—and often, without crime.

State Responsibility for Juvenile Detention Care, Youth Development and Delinquency Prevention Administration, HEW, 1970

The resulting reports ranged from descriptions of "a very frightening and demoralizing place" to a detention center where "the children seemed happy (under the circumstances)." What became clear is that each community must look to its own detention centers to see what description fits and to learn what is being done for or to children in trouble. The descriptions from individual Sections of their own communities speak for themselves in introducing the subject of detention:

Once in the detention center, the children lose their identity. They wear institutional clothing, eat institutional food, think and do in the way of the institution. There is no therapy; they may see a caseworker for a few minutes. . . . We did not see any children shackled to the beds or being beaten. But we also did not see any evidence of constructive work being done with the children. It is a very frightening and demoralizing place. It has been said that if a child is not a murderer or drug addict when he enters, he may well be after repeated times at the home. . . . The one improvement that I can see over the past ten years is that now infants, toddlers, and young children are not sent there.

It was a very impersonal building, but in all fairness, I must say that the few staff members were extremely kind, dedicated, cooperative, and receptive. . . . The facility contains an open circular room where boys and girls eat and play (ping pong, pool, etc.), a classroom where one teacher attempts to teach approximately eleven students, all of whom have fallen behind in their studies and all of whom are at a different level of study. At night, boys and girls are locked in special small cells (some have sinks, others just a bed). The time lock then releases them in the morning. There is an inter-communication system if one of the children needs help, consultation, or becomes ill. At night, there is a part-time employed couple on duty available if a child needs help with a problem. . . . All belongings are locked and must be asked for. . . . The center was clean and the children seemed happy (under the circumstances). I tried to talk to a couple of the kids and they seemed polite, aloof, and uninterested.

The center is overcrowded, staff turnover is great, many untrained, salaries are low. . . . Juveniles are assigned to rooms by age and sex. Nature of crime is not a factor. There is little or no privacy or freedom. All girls on admittance must undergo pelvic examination to determine if they are pregnant as no institution will take pregnant girls. Also, all children must go through the Cuprex Delouse test—yellow, burning substance sprayed on bodies. This is done in a group. . . . Our interviewer found the atmosphere to be that of a jail, monotonous, and very regimented. Physical conditions were barely adequate, due mainly to overcrowding. Children have to sleep on floors if rooms are filled. Some of the staff seemed aware of shortcomings but not all agreed that change and improvements are needed. This facility has been rated in the top five percent of all detention centers in the U.S. based on physical structure, quality of staff, and percent of recidivism (48%).

We were deeply depressed by the general appearance and condition of the entire building. It was dreary, unattractive and actually many of the bedrooms were not fit for a reasonable level of human comfort. In one room there were wall-to-wall cots and windows were covered with blankets to try to keep out the cold. All 'social' rooms were barren with little, if any, comforts. There was an inadequate area for physical activity. Most children who were there at the time of our visit seemed lethargic and disinterested; not actively involved in anything constructive. The only two pleasant rooms in the building were closed because of lack of staff.

This detention center for girls is housed in a building that should have been condemned fifty years ago. There are huge cracks in the walls and ceilings. Water seeps through many of them because of the condition of the plumbing. We had to sidestep puddles in the hallways. The so-called gymnasium is a basement room with so many structural pillars that no real physical activity is possible. In their dormitories, the girls each have a 'cubby' in which clothing and personal possessions are kept, explaining the generally disheveled look of their clothes. Many of the girls seemed to be slightly sedated, an impression confirmed by a member of the staff who cited heavy reliance on tranquilizers. Questioned about homosexuality among the girls, he said it was a misunderstood phenomenon: 'They're just looking for families.' (This detention center has since been closed.)

One step toward improving conditions may lie in the adoption of a National Advisory Commission recommendation that "Every detention facility for adults or juveniles should have provisions for an outside, objective evaluation at least once a year." This need for monitoring is emphasized by the fact that fourteen states have no laws requiring regular inspection of juvenile detention centers, and many states which do have such laws make no provision for compliance with recommendations arising from such inspection.*

As pointed out in Connecticut's 1971 Juvenile Court Manual, *"loss of liberty in any form is a serious matter."* The loss is compounded when children are unnecessarily detained while waiting for adjudication, further compounded when the conditions are punishing, compounded intolerably when the children are only accused of such status offenses as playing hooky and run-

*Statewide Jail Standards and Inspection Systems Project, American Bar Association, Commission on Correctional Facilities and Services.

ning away, or when children are themselves victims of parental anger, neglect, or crimes and the community is unable to find a place for them.

In community after community, detention centers were found to be places where the seriousness of losing liberty was not treated with the same gravity for children as for adults. The decision to detain was found to be a police as well as court power, particularly when no court or probation official was available. This was usually the case when juveniles were picked up late at night or on weekends—those periods which are also most likely to produce juvenile mischief. Police discretion on arresting or not arresting a child is thereby extended to release or detention as well, with detention less likely where children have backup from parents. Detention is liable to be used as a tactic in combatting delinquency as illustrated in two West Coast suburbs. When delinquency increased, orders went out to the police to detain almost every child on his second offense.

Yet, when proper criteria are applied, no more than 10 percent of all children arrested by police require detention according to the National Council on Crime and Delinquency. Secure custody, they maintain, is necessary only: (1) If the child is almost certain to run away while the court is handling the case; (2) If the child is almost certain to commit an offense dangerous to himself or the community before court disposition of his case; (3) If the child must be held for another jurisdiction.

In practice, as government studies have reported and as the NCJW study documented, detention is misused, abused, and over-used. This was reflected in the proportion of juveniles detained on charges for which only children can be arrested—status offenses. Of 42 reports containing information on this point, 10 said "all" or "most" of the children in the detention centers visited were status offenders; in another 14, the proportion of status offenders varied from over 40 percent to 90 percent. At one center, when the director was asked how many of the 30 children there really needed to be detained, he reviewed each case separately, then answered, "Two." In another city, a 1968-1970 study of youths held in the detention center revealed that only three percent were charged with major offenses against persons.

Percentages, proportions, and estimates blur the harsh reality that flesh-and-blood children fill detention centers. NCJW members reflected the reality in their strong reactions after direct observation and in the specific cases they cited. For example: a 15-year-old girl who ended up in a mental institution because she wanted to escape the horrors of a detention center. It is noteworthy only as something that literally could have happened to any teenager.

Once this girl's case entered the process of juvenile justice, understandable teenage rebellion was escalated to personal calamity. Her parents had divorced and she was living with her father and stepmother, whom she resented. High-strung and emotional, the girl began staying out at night past her father's curfew as an expression of her resentment. He kept warning her. She kept staying out late. He decided to teach her a lesson by calling the police and reporting her missing one night when she was still out at midnight. When the police brought her home, the father refused to allow her in and declared her out of parental control.

The police in that community had no place to take her but a detention facility with locked doors and barred windows. She was put in a room with drug addicts and prostitutes. Distraught and desperate to get out, she asked the advice of a fellow inmate who said that if she attempted suicide she would get out. But she didn't say where the girl would go. So the teenager used a nail file to slash her wrists, the attendant was called, and the girl taken to a mental institution. Fortunately, her stab wounds were superficial. It took the girl's father three months to get her out.

To one degree or other, that teenager's trauma

can be reconstructed for any child caught in the detention experience, bearing in mind that distinctions usually are not made for the alleged offense committed by the juvenile. (Over four-fifths of the NCJW reports providing data on this point said that no separation was made by type of offense.) The child enters detention in an upset condition, and an institutional identity is thrust upon him. He is depersonalized. His possessions are taken away. He is assigned sleeping quarters which are either so crowded that he lacks privacy entirely or put overnight into a room, all alone, with the door locked. He is faced with a standardized routine and a set of regulations. All euphemisms aside, it feels like jail and, for all purposes, it is a jail for children. In some communities, children are handcuffed when brought to court from detention, even if the charge is truancy. One administrator offered the explanation that it reduces the temptation to try to impress the other youngsters or to run away.

All children, some more than others, are vulnerable to such an experience. They are searching for identity and struggling to establish a self-image, a struggle that is more acute for children in trouble. Then they encounter custodial handling by those in authority who put them under lock and key, with the implied judgment of guilt. If the label is bad and seems to be stamped on youngsters at a detention center, why not live up to it?

Each year, some 500,000 youngsters in the United States wait varying lengths of time in detention centers, and another 100,000 have the jolting experience of being detained in adult jails. Many get out after a short stay—overnight or a few days. For others, "temporary" detention lasts weeks and even months. These include children who have done nothing serious enough to be sent away to a training institution, but who must wait for a place to go. (Such as a 14-year-old with an I.Q. of 156 and a light history of truancy and behavior problems who was thrown out of the house by his parents.

When seen, he had already spent 83 days in detention while a place was sought for him.) Extended detention is the fate of children who are victims of crimes, children who have been raped or sodomized by their parents.

No reliable generalization can be made nationally about the amount of time children spend in detention centers. According to an analysis of juvenile codes issued by the National Assessment of Juvenile Correction, only eleven states have enacted statutes limiting the pre-adjudicatory detention period. These few range from three to ninety days. Children are being kept too long in the punishing limbo of detention in spite of legal restrictions on length of stay. In one community, where the limit is two weeks, children "linger indefinitely" in the detention center if their parents will not or cannot take them home. In another facility, where the legal maximum is 90 days, "hard to place" children may stay for a full year. The accepted criteria for detention practices are: a court hearing within 48 hours of detention, disposition of the case within 15 days if the child is held in custody, within 30 days if released to a parent or guardian.

The most positive description of a detention center visited comes from a Midwest Section. As described by NCJW observers, the center tries to avoid confining children, following the philosophy of juvenile court that "no child should have his liberty curtailed if there is an alternative open to the court." The center operates a 24-hour screening unit manned by staffers with degrees in social work or related fields, and considerable experience in working with troubled juveniles. After a policeman brings a youngster to the center and all pertinent information is taken down, the admissions staff tries to locate the parents, if the police have been unsuccessful in their attempts to do so. Most youngsters are released to their parents. Those who have committed no offenses and will not or cannot return home are sent to foster homes. Some can be placed in a Volunteers of

Detention as Punishment

America shelter. It should be noted that although this description is generally favorable, it must be considered in the context of ideal procedures as outlined in Chapter 8.

In deciding whether to detain a child, the staff considers attitude, seriousness of offense, and whether the child will appear in court if summoned. If juveniles are detained, their records are sent immediately to court intake so their case can be expedited. No child can be detained more than six court hours (excluding weekends and holidays) without a detention hearing and no more than 12 court hours unless a petition has been filed and a judge or referee decides that the child should remain in custody. To make certain no child is forgotten, a new detention hearing must be held every ten days.

Under this system, most children stay only a few days; the average stay is 4.8 days. Those in detention live in a 30-bed center built in 1957 and remodeled in 1970 to add 29 beds, a gymnasium and new classrooms. It is composed of three levels: the lower level contains a large, cheerful cafeteria, gymnasium and classrooms, a second level consists of a large recreation room, counselors' offices and girls' living quarters; the third level houses the boys' sleeping quarters.

An effort is made to avoid depersonalization. Once a child is examined and takes a shower, he is allowed to wear his own clothes. A chaplain assigned to the center, working with a group of pastors learning clinical counseling, talks to the youngsters and holds voluntary interdenominational services on Sunday. Volunteers tutor youngsters and provide contact with an outsider who will listen to them. The classrooms are small and intimate; bulletin boards and windows are covered with children's work. Art projects done in the art classes are displayed throughout the building and even adorn the waiting room at juvenile court.

The atmosphere of the center and the attitudes of the staff were described by NCJW observers.

There are many bulletin boards on the walls and the children are encouraged to write down their thoughts and post them. Music (the kind children like) can be heard in many places throughout the building. All of the staff in the center have been trained to work with troubled youth and are encouraged to provide as much warmth and support as possible. . . . The counselors are young people, college-educated in child care, psychology or sociology. They talk with the children, supervise their activities, and keep a log on each child's actions, attitudes, and problems as he spends his time awaiting a court hearing. Disruptive children receive extra help from the counselors, who have written guidelines to assist them in handling behavior problems.

Nonetheless, in this facility, as in the typical detention center, security means locked doors. From 10:30 p.m. until 7 a.m., each child is in his own room and the door is locked. An intercom system enables him to ask for the aid of a counselor if necessary. Corridor doors are locked night and day, and permission is required to go from one part of the building to the other. Even substantial professional services delivered in a compassionate manner cannot erase for the child the essential fact that he is locked up.

Security is a recurrent theme in reports on detention centers. One report from a southern city stated: "All detention is 'secure' in that doors are kept locked, and even when going to the bathroom there is always a guard in attendance. No toilet facilities have doors, so that there is no privacy." In upstate New York, a new director of a new facility noted that security is considered first and all else comes after, adding, "We are concerned with protecting the child and the community."

Surveillance extends to visitation and usually to mail. In one Midwest center, children are given a handbook which tells them about regulations and even more about the detention-center approach. On the one hand, the children read: "We think all people are important. This makes you important. . . . We really feel YOU *are important.*" This appears opposite a page which advises juveniles that all letters must be placed in an unsealed envelope which then goes to the probation officer handling his case: "If something in the letter is not clear, the probation officer may talk to you about it. Your assigned probation officer will read all of the mail that comes to you before giving it to you."

To encourage cooperative behavior, some detention centers use incentive programs. One center places youngsters in one of three groups—A, B, or C—depending on behavior. The A group gets the most privileges, including later hours and Saturday night pizza with the staff. A more usual approach involves "rewards" such as trips to town and movies or the earning of "merit" points that can be turned into treats at the canteen. (Such rewards raise questions about average length of stay.) No significant evidence was found of corporal punishment; isolation is used for recalcitrant youngsters. Its official use varied from one center where isolation lasted from five or ten minutes to three or four hours, depending upon change of attitude and behavior, to another center with a 24-hour maximum in isolation. In the latter instance, the staff checks the child every 15 minutes. In more than one instance, however, staff revealed broad discretion in the use of "solitary." One attorney described staff's placing a child in isolation, removing him before the lapse of the official 24-hour limit, only to return him after a brief respite.

What emerges from inspection of detention centers and their many variations is an uncertain, uneasy, and uneven interplay between the need for security and the needs of children. It is complicated by the constant turnover of youngsters and the differences in reasons for detaining them. A Midwest Section report stated:

The constantly changing population of the center with resulting psychological and physical problems of trying to work with many situations on a short-term basis must greatly frustrate the staff. The children usually resent being detained. They range from the frightened child who is a runaway or a drug user to the more sophisticated youths who have committed felonies and have appeared in court many times. Most of the girls who stay in the center are there because of family problems and are not segregated from more sophisticated offenders. There is a certain contagion factor involved, which the counselors try to minimize through program planning.

Shortages of money and of qualified personnel are cited as recurring problems. The money problem tends to squeeze out aspects that involve recreation and extra services and to reduce the centers to their custodial function. Depending on the community, the qualifications for personnel range from degrees in social work or the social sciences to high school diplomas. A more significant factor is harder to pinpoint and that is the staff attitude, which reflects the policies of the director who hired the personnel.

Because attitude is an intangible, there is no substitute for first-hand observation. In various instances, the reports cited the warm, positive attitude of directors and staff. Observers were also able to sense the gap between what was said and what was the actual atmosphere. One director stressed that he wanted to give the children the feeling that the detention center was "a home away from home" and that he and his wife were "just like parents—and in some cases better." NCJW observers questioned his description: "We felt that all was not well. The children that we saw seemed to be sitting around aimlessly watching TV or doing nothing. When asked about this, the director didn't seem to be too concerned or interested. In fact, he was very curt to one child who asked a question. The general feeling was one of fear of the director."

Detention as Punishment

Volunteers perform a variety of roles in detention centers, with a number of centers reporting a greater need for them. Of 66 detention centers in which the question of volunteers was explored, about three-fourths draw on volunteers. Volunteers provide tutoring, recreation, and supportive services. Typical reports on their role: "Volunteers are an important part of the program and provide tutors for children having trouble with their school work." . . . "Volunteers come occasionally and give holiday parties and bring books, magazines, and treats. This is important because last year, only three of 19 children detained at Christmas had a visit from family or friends of their own." . . . "The greatest need volunteer-wise is for volunteers to work on a one-to-one basis with the juveniles." . . . "The probation counselors indicated an interest in having volunteers act as consistent and close contacts for juvenile and family." . . . "This program consists of big brother and sister volunteers and foster grandparents."

But, although volunteer services may improve conditions for children in detention centers, they are no substitute for system change. In a number of states, therefore, NCJW Sections have given public testimony regarding the need for smaller detention centers, shelter care, better physical facilities, time limits on detention, and services to children in their own homes as alternatives to detention.

A recurrent theme in Section reports relates to the need to create alternatives so that detention will be reduced to an absolute minimum. The Justice For Children Task Force has urged that around-the-clock intake services could dispose of many cases on the spot, eliminating the practice of detaining a child for a day or two before sending him home. It would end the contagious mixing of children whose minor infractions do not warrant detention with those few who are truly dangerous to themselves and others.

In NCJW interviews, many police, court and detention personnel expressed frustration with the lack of resources available to the child who is abused or not wanted at home. Too often, they said, the only door open is the detention center's. As a result, typical Section findings included:

We found immediate need for crisis centers and halfway houses in the area for the status offender, first offender, and seriously disturbed child who cannot be taken home due to a family in crisis, or lack of responsible parent/guardian/custodian. (South)

There is a critical need for short-term-stay facilities ranging from one night to six weeks. Presently there is much resistance by community to this operation. (Midwest)

Detention is not supposed to be used for temporary sheltering care. Nevertheless . . . they are forced to use the detention home for children awaiting placement in group homes, boarding schools and treatment centers because of a lack of adequate shelter care facilities. . . . A city policeman said that a child may be placed in detention when the parents are so angry that the police are afraid for the child's safety if he were released to their custody. (Northeast)

Minimizing the use of detention requires community alternatives such as group homes, temporary foster homes, detention boarding homes, and neighborhood supervision. Besides the all-important human factor, the cost factor argues for such alternatives. Detention centers have been estimated at costing between $20,000 and $35,000 per bed to build (an estimate that must be revised upward in the face of soaring building costs). Cost per child per day runs between $20 and $35. To cite one comparison: a program for detention boarding homes in upstate New York costs $6 per child per day.

Detention as Punishment

From various parts of the country, NCJW Sections have reported on the success of these alternatives to detention centers:

TEMPORARY FOSTER HOMES—At about one-half the cost of institutional care, children are placed with families who take care of them until long-term arrangements are made. In one New England community, volunteers take into their homes children who are considered "low risks," often runaways. Children can be sheltered in these homes without parental consent with appropriate orders from the juvenile court.

DETENTION BOARDING HOMES—As a form of non-secure detention, boarding homes are licensed and are under the supervision of juvenile authorities. Space is kept available on a standby basis and boarding home parents are paid according to a schedule that is increased when a child is placed there. In an upstate New York community, where six detention boarding homes operate, the parents vary widely in age from a couple in their late twenties to a grandmother. They maintain the same standards as foster homes, with boarding home mothers not permitted to work outside their homes. The children continue to attend their regular school, if possible; otherwise a school near the boarding home. The program, operating since 1967, has kept children for as long as six months in such homes; recently a state ruling limited the stay to 45 days. Observers found this indication of the program's success: "Sometimes the children have to leave the boarding home when they much prefer to remain there."

NEIGHBORHOOD SUPERVISION—A program for supervising alleged delinquents enables them to live at home or in foster homes while the court disposes of their case. College students, housewives, and senior citizens have been used in such programs in different parts of the country. A St. Louis pilot project was found to be particularly successful. Community Youth Leaders were recruited from the neighborhoods in which the children were living and they supervised youngsters facing court action. The dropout rate was nil, the cost was considerably less than in an institution, and the rate of new delinquencies was far below that of children held in detention centers.

In Massachusetts, where statewide action was taken to close down all detention centers, a visit to one of the last remaining centers brought this reaction: "This facility, especially in contrast with the newer group homes and halfway houses, serves as a reminder of the deplorable conditions juveniles were exposed to under the archaic system of juvenile justice." After meeting with the director and his assistant following a tour of the facility, "it was easy to see why they both were primarily aiming for an eventual shutdown of the center as it now functions."

New Jersey has moved in the same direction with a new juvenile justice code that went into effect on March 1, 1974. Counties were barred from sending status offenders to detention facilities for juvenile delinquents. New facilities were ordered with an open-door rather than a locked-door policy. The shelters could not be physically restricting, allowing free access to the community. The head of the State Department of Institutions and Agencies described the ideal shelter as housing six to eight youths for periods of about two weeks or less, with the youngsters encouraged to attend local schools. Or a better solution: temporary foster homes.

Thus, in the interplay between the need of security and the needs of children, signs of revision can be identified. Current reassessment of secure detention has created a demand to put security in its very limited place and not to impose it unnecessarily on the majority of children in trouble. Communities are being challenged to emphasize the needs and rights of those children who await their day in court.

4 Children in Court

In a large city, the walls of juvenile court are lined with children. They are there at all hours of the day, "waiting seemingly endless amounts of time for their turns to come—for the people who work in this big, grey building to make a decision that may well affect the rest of their lives." Coming for the first time, they are "frightened, bewildered by the hugeness and the people and the forms and the papers . . ." The confusing sight also confounded uninitiated observers, who asked: How much more confused must children be?

Whether in metropolis or county seat, juvenile court is a court in search of its appropriate role—as far as children, parents, community, and justice are concerned. Ever since the first one opened in Cook County, Illinois, on July 1, 1899, juvenile courts have been both legal and social instruments. They were set up as more than courts of law in which, as noted in the *Harvard Law Review* in 1909, the judge would determine what is best done in the juvenile's "interest and in the interest of the state to save him from a downward career."

The juvenile court judge, chief actor in this

search, is under pressure from the community to play many parts: psychologist, pediatrician, police officer, social worker, welfare worker, family counselor, legal expert, judicial referee, special pleader, neutral arbitrator, man or woman in the middle of many failures. In a report entitled *Juvenile Justice Confounded*, Justine Wise Polier, former New York State Family Court Judge, has pointed out the "pathology" in a situation where mental health services nationwide are "appalling." The courts throughout the country "are confronted not only by the pathology of the child and his family, but by the community pathology that denies treatment services to those children who are most in need."*

As set forth by the National Council of Juvenile Court Judges, the judge and the juvenile court must balance three primary obligations: (1) to protect the community; (2) to act in the best interest and welfare of the child; (3) to uphold the dignity of the law and the public's faith in the judicial system.

Achieving this balance is not easy. In many communities the court has been assigned the role, which Atlanta Section's report describes as "the conscience of society rather than the interpreter and implementer of a specific set of laws."

Across the country, when NCJW volunteers visited the courts and talked to judges, they found them responsive and articulate. For the most part, judges emphasized their concern for the "best interests" of children. Their fatherly approach reflected the traditional *parens patriae* orientation of juvenile court; they saw themselves acting as surrogate parents doing what was best for the children coming before them. This was reflected in the tendency of judges to talk in an intimate way to children in the course of otherwise businesslike proceedings far removed from the children's understanding or participation.

Juvenile Justice Confounded: Pretensions and Realities of Treatment Services. Committee on Mental Health Services Inside and Outside the Family Court in the City of New York, 1972, p. 5.

Children in Court

In a juvenile court in which the NCJW observer described the judge as "white, middle-class and secure" and most of the children before him as "black, impoverished and scared," the mixing of the paternal role with the judicial was summed up by the judge. When asked if children are charged with offenses that would not be offenses if committed by adults, the judge promptly replied: "Of course, but somebody has to supervise them."

After sifting reports from across the country, the NCJW Task Force pinpointed inconsistencies that surfaced:

Judges' favorable descriptions of what happened in their own courtrooms frequently were different from what was actually observed.

Judges were concerned about the lack of community resources, but rarely used their influence and authority to encourage the community to develop facilities and resources.

Judges for the most part failed to visit regularly the various facilities to which they send children, thereby ignoring a practice that would increase awareness of what their decisions mean in the lives of children.

Individualized justice is considered the heart of the juvenile system, but in practice, limited facilities and alternatives dictate the decisions; too often "the best interests of the child" cannot be met through the choices available to the court.

Juvenile courts place both adjudication and disposition in the hands of a judge. At adjudication he conducts a trial of the charges, hears evidence and witnesses, and decides the case. If the judge discharges (acquits) the child, the case goes no further. Otherwise, it goes to the stage of disposition, where the judge determines what action is to be taken. The child may be sent to a training institution, placed on probation, or referred for treatment or services at home or in a community-based facility, if one exists.

For a child in the docket, the court's discretionary power is awesome, the exercise of it up to the individual judge. He has the choice of following laws of evidence strictly and deciding a case on the basis of the facts as presented in court, or deciding on the basis of the whole child and what is best for him or her. Drawing on her extensive experience as a lawyer in juvenile court, Judge Lois Forer comments: "Faced with the dilemma between a strict due-process trial and doing what is best for the child, many judges try to do a little of both."

In recent years, the U.S. Supreme Court has laid down guidelines on the adjudicatory (fact-finding) half of juvenile court operations. The thrust of three key decisions was expressed in the first of them when the majority decision noted "grounds for concern that the child receives the worst of both worlds; that he gets neither the protection accorded to adults nor the solicitous care and regenerative treatment postulated for children."*

Across the country, NCJW looked for the impact on juvenile justice of these Supreme Court decisions which ruled that "neither the Fourteenth Amendment nor the Bill of Rights is for adults alone." In essence, here is what the Supreme Court had decided:

KENT DECISION (1966)—Procedures were established for waiving jurisdiction by juvenile court when a youngster is "suspected of serious crimes." Before a juvenile case can be shifted to criminal court, a hearing must be held that measures up to the legal standards of due process and fair treatment. In such a hearing, a juvenile is entitled to legal counsel. This decision foreshadowed the next two.

GAULT DECISION (1967)—Whenever juveniles are accused of violating a criminal statute (felony or misdemeanor) and face commitment to an institution, they must have due process in juvenile court. That

*Kent v. United States, 383 U.S. 541, 556 (1966).

means a notice of the charges, the right to counsel, the right to confront and cross-examine witnesses and the privilege against self-incrimination. (In the case of Arizona teenager Gerald Gault, which produced this decision, none of this protection was provided a 15-year-old accused of making an obscene phone call. No lawyer. No witnesses called. No transcript of the hearing. If he were 18, he could have been fined $5 to $50 and been jailed for not more than two months. As a juvenile, he was sent to the State Industrial School until he was 21, where he spent two years before the Supreme Court freed him.)

WINSHIP DECISION (1970)—When juveniles are charged with actions that would be a crime for an adult, the charges must be proved beyond a reasonable doubt.

On the key point of providing legal counsel for juveniles, significant headway was reported by NCJW observers. Of reports on this point, almost 70 percent found that children were provided with counsel. Of the remainder, half found that counsel was provided when requested. But implementation varied greatly: from those courts where counsel was "automatic" to those where it is "offered but not often used" to those where it is "not provided" at all.

In one major city, a lack of funds for lawyers coupled with the requirement that lawyers be assigned in court led to a backlog of more than 4,000 cases. This situation creates two serious problems: large numbers of children are warehoused in detention facilities awaiting trial, and lawyers have inadequate time to meet with their clients to prepare for court. Several NCJW Sections have become involved in efforts to secure financial support for adequate legal services for the poor. For example, Indianapolis Section was among those that fought for continued funding of a public defender service whose two full-time attorneys and twenty interns represented 1,000 indigent children in one year.

In another city, when a juvenile court judge was

asked why 95 percent of the cases waived the right to counsel, he replied: "They have confidence in the court." By contrast, in New York City where the work of Legal Aid Society's Juvenile Rights Division is praised for its efforts to safeguard children's rights, its lawyers, called law guardians, represent nearly all children appearing before the court as status offenders or as delinquents.

In most communities, free counsel is available to children whose families cannot afford a lawyer, although they are not always informed of this. A usual procedure is for the court to appoint counsel from a pool of lawyers in private practice to work on a per diem basis. Since most lawyers handle juvenile cases part-time, they are often ill-attuned to the legal/social atmosphere of juvenile court. The lawyer, after all, is trained in the adversary role of fighting for his client.

Insofar as juvenile court judges tend toward a fatherly approach, the lawyer appears on the scene with a different perspective. Typically, he has been handed a social problem in a legal form and is carrying on a legal fight in a quasi-legal arena. Chagrined, one lawyer said, "I never know if I'm helping a kid—or hurting him—by getting him off." When being judged delinquent is the only way a community will offer needed services to a juvenile, a community's failure becomes an attorney's dilemma.

In sizing up the problem of representing children, some lawyers aimed their criticisms at the bench: "Judges are not sensitive to the needs of children because they are more concerned with moving cases to another department". . . . "After being forced to begin appointing counsel, the juvenile judges have managed to round up a group of lawyers who will be happy to just stand up in court (or lie down) while children are committed". . . . "The biggest problem I face in trying to provide good legal counsel for juveniles is judicial apathy. This, however, is simply a mirror of the general apathy that is demonstrated by almost every level of society with which I have dealt concerning juveniles."

From the viewpoint of judge and probation officer, the lawyer can seem like an enemy force, even acting against his own client's best interests. In one court, NCJW observers heard complaints that the lawyers representing juveniles "interfere" with the court. It was claimed they "not only slowed down the legal process, but that they would do anything to get the children back on the street." A lawyer, describing his side of the coin, told an NCJW observer in another court that it is the judge's job, not his, to decide whether a juvenile should be institutionalized. But, he noted, that most clients are not helped by being confined in the kind of institutions that exist. Another lawyer, admitting that he knew nothing about the juvenile justice system as a whole, said: "I just try, as most other lawyers do, to win my case on legal points. I depend on the Probation Office to take care of the child and do the investigation."

In one statewide guide for juvenile court judges, the judge-author advises attorneys to be always guided by what is best for the juvenile client, including whether to plead guilty. "In delinquency proceedings," the guide advises, "attorneys who advise guilty children to remain silent and demand that the child's guilt be proven 'beyond a reasonable doubt and to a moral certainty' may be doing their clients a disservice." Thus, for lawyer, as for judge, a day in juvenile court can mean searching for the appropriate role under the circumstances.

Lawyers in juvenile court frequently lack the opportunity to see the "whole child." Several NCJW community reports expressed concern about the limited contact between lawyer and juvenile client. Often, it amounts only to a few minutes of conversation in a court waiting room just before the case is called.

For their part, most judges complained that their caseloads are too large. Many told NCJW observers that they do not have enough time to devote to the cases that pile up in front of them. The actual time devoted to cases had a staggering variation—from two minutes to six hours. For those courts in which the length of the average hearing was recorded, more than half were 15 minutes or less. In less than one-fifth of the courts did the average hearing last as long as an hour. Observers also cited the remarks of juvenile court judges in metropolitan areas, as reported in the press. One said he averaged six minutes a case, another remarked that judges are forced to make "snap decisions."

To carry on their many-sided role, juvenile court judges have little or no special training. The typical response in individual reports on the question of special training for juvenile court judges was "none." Where special training is available, as that provided by the National Council of Juvenile Court Judges, it is usually up to the individual judge to take advantage of it. While juvenile court judges are usually lawyers, this is not always the case. A survey by the National Council of Juvenile Court Judges in 1973 found that 82.4 percent of the juvenile court judges had three or more years of legal education, as compared to 69.1 percent in 1963.

Part of the problem of upgrading judges' qualifications is related to the status of the juvenile court itself. In many communities studied, it lacks the prestige of other courts, particularly within the legal profession. This lack is reflected in lower salaries, inadequate resources and high turnover of court personnel. Growing awareness of the social costs of delinquency, coupled with general court reform efforts, are beginning to result in shifts in juvenile court organization. Among those reported were: establishment of separate, full-time juvenile courts; longer term assignments of judges to juvenile courts; a broadening of court jurisdiction from juvenile to family matters; and the elevation of juvenile court administration from a local to circuit or state level.

Overall, the need for specialized training has

been cited as deserving the "highest priority" by Illinois Congressman Tom Railsback of the House Judiciary Committee. In referring to proposed legislation for an Institute for Juvenile Justice, he told the NCJW Joint Program Institute in January 1974: "Judges, parole officers, policemen, social workers—all must learn how to deal with young people who enter and leave the juvenile justice system and try to readjust to society."

Reports on the practice of visiting juvenile facilities regularly were disappointing. Judges tend to visit detention facilities more than others, possibly because they are usually located near the court. Slightly more than half of the reports said judges visit detention centers regularly. However, only 28 percent and 31 percent reported regular visits to training schools and shelters respectively.

In New York City, the judge in charge of administering family court conducted a "consciousness-raising tour" for judges in June 1974. Judge Joseph B. Williams led the eight-hour tour of poverty neighborhoods and youth care facilities to make his colleagues more aware of where children in court come from and where the court sends them.

While juvenile court judges in large cities devote themselves full-time to juvenile matters, in smaller cities and towns such duties are part-time. The survey by the National Council of Juvenile Court Judges found that most judges spend one-fourth or less of their time with juvenile matters. Even where juvenile court judges are assigned full-time, they can be overwhelmed by cases, such as the single judge handling juvenile cases for a Southern city of a half million. NCJW observers found that rural juvenile court judges must cover so wide a geographical area that they are often inaccessible to individual communities.

The situation places pressure on juvenile court in its attempt to provide a prompt hearing and disposition for children languishing in detention. In over three-fourths of the courts reported on, a hearing is held within 48 hours. However, in many communities the 48 hours is stretched when weekends and holidays intervene. One of the worst examples was in a large city with only one juvenile judge; sometimes one month elapses before even a hearing takes place.

A high proportion of the courts disposed of the cases within the period of time recommended at the 1970 White House Conference on Children. Where youngsters are held in custody, in about 70 percent of the courts a dispositional hearing is held within 15 judicial days. Where youngsters are released in the custody of parents or guardians, such hearings are held within 30 days in about 60 percent of the courts visited.

Perhaps as a result of recent Supreme Court rulings, children in court are receiving increased protection under the Bill of Rights and the Fourteenth Amendment. In almost all courts, children and their families are given notice of charges, something that was not done in the Gault case. In three-fourths of the courts, children had the privilege against self-incrimination. However, this protection is rarely extended to statements made at intake.

Moreover, most courts are following the recommended practice of separating the fact-finding of adjudication from the fateful decisions involved in disposition of the case. Some 70 percent are separating the two hearings. This, in effect, enables the court to stress its legal side in deciding the facts of the case and its social side in deciding the fate of the child.

A *Handbook for New Juvenile Court Judges*, prepared by the National Council of Juvenile Court Judges, suggests the quality of the dispositional hearing: The special needs of the child "become the subject of the dispositional phase of the proceedings, and Gault, other than its doctrine of fundamental fairness, is no longer a consideration." Thus, in the disposition process, "the heartbeat of juvenile court" in individualized justice can be heard.

Children in Court

At the dispositional hearing, juvenile court judges confront the fundamental dilemma of their position. They must cope with the "delinquency" of parents and of community in deciding what to do with the children in front of them. One Midwest Section of NCJW raised a question that is not merely rhetorical: "Can judges be as wise as King Solomon?"

NCJW observers from various parts of the country illustrated the dilemmas of the juvenile courtroom with illustrations that struck them. For instance:

She was going to be 14 next day. She had been placed before in a foster home where she'd been getting on well and making B's in schoolwork. But they couldn't keep her any longer and sent her back home. Her mother called the police to take her because they couldn't get along. You could see the judge was upset and had trouble deciding what to do with her. She was committed to a training institution. I could have cried.

A fourteen-year-old lives in a foster home, three miles from her natural parents. Occasionally she visits her mentally ill mother and younger brothers and sisters. Her father asks the court to have the girl moved to a foster home that is farther away because her visits have a disturbing effect on her mother and the younger children.

A 13 or 14-year-old girl was brought to court by her mother who claimed she was out of control. The mother said the girl wouldn't listen, and she couldn't deal with her. Because the mother refused to take the child home and because no private placement was found, the girl was being locked up in a detention facility. It was our impression that the mother did not want her at home for some reason that had nothing to do with the girl's behavior, that the mother had a boyfriend or several boyfriends and her daughter was not welcome with the men present. This seemed clear because the mother never cited anything specific against her daughter. The child wanted very much to go home. She promised to be good and begged her mother to take her home. But the mother absolutely refused to do so. The judge had no choice. If he made the mother take the child home, she would be back in ten days, once again claiming that her child was incorrigible. The judge was left in the position of trying to find placement for a child in a situation like this, something that is not easy to come by. Finally, the girl was led from the court crying, resisting the officers, who were taking her back to a locked detention facility. The child kept saying, 'Please take me home.' The mother did not say a word. She turned and walked out of the court.

At a dispositional hearing that lasted 25 minutes, the judge followed the probation officer's recommendation that Richard, who was 17, be permitted to remain at home and have counseling or pay $50 if he didn't complete the counseling. The boy denied the charges in the probation officer's report that he had had a few beers before disturbing the peace. The judge became very upset at this, explained what perjury was, and suggested that perhaps they should have the probation officer come to court for a confrontation because 'I won't tolerate lying in court.' Richard's attitude was defiant and smirking, but when warned of a perjury charge, he changed his story. His father was saying that he was a good boy and that he obeyed him. The judge said, 'I'm not here to punish your son but to try to help him. The first step is for him to realize his problems. The underlying problem is his drinking (he was arrested three times for drunkenness, starting at age 12), and I'd like to offer him counseling as an alternative to his fine.' The father seemed most concerned about the $50 fine, but the judge stressed it was not his responsibility, but the boy's, to make the payment—no matter how long it would take—if he did not participate in the counseling program. The judge expressed his doubts—in court and afterwards when father and son had left court—that the recommendation to *send the boy home may not have been the best one in this case.*

A particularly vivid description of a busy juvenile court was provided by observers in a large city who reported that it took "three court visits and many questions" just to identify the various people in the courtroom. They depicted the court as "confusing, congested, and complicated," as "buried under a morass of papers, folders, and reports," and as "in a constant state of siege by armies of people going in and out of courtrooms and elevators." The report continued:

One of the groups of people, shuffling from place to place, finally end up waiting on long wooden benches outside the courtroom. The atmosphere and general attitude is slightly less imposing and about as friendly as the waiting room at Grand Central Station. The noise at times approaches a decibel level that makes it impossible to hear inside the courtroom.

Within the courtroom, the procedures seem to be an exercise by friendly equals in the same profession, while the petitioners, as outsiders, remain mute and unknowing. The insiders include judge, clerk, recorder, liaison probation officer, prosecuting counsel, defense counsel, uniformed court officers, representatives of the various social services, and interpreters, almost all of whom are constantly in motion.

That description on the East Coast was echoed by another on the West Coast. The juvenile court building "was extremely crowded, with much confusion. There was an information desk staffed by men in sheriff's department uniforms, but no one approached it for help. There were rows of hard benches along the halls, and they were packed, standing room only." In one courtroom, the judge appeared, but no court recorder did, so all scheduled hearings were cancelled. The same thing happened in two other courtrooms that day. In another courtroom, NCJW observers were taken aback by the reason for postponing a case: "the court had the wrong petition for the juvenile; there were witnesses to testify against him on robbery and car-stripping charges, but the complaint was for joy-riding, for which there were no witnesses present."

The juvenile court in a medium-sized New England city offered a contrasting impression. The atmosphere, observers reported, was "informal but concerned and respectful, . . . not confusing and high-powered." The rights of juveniles were carefully safeguarded, with lawyers provided for all except those who waived counsel. An interpreter was available for non-English-speaking children and parents and school and church officials were present for various cases. Social workers who worked with the families were on hand as well as probation officers who "seemed well acquainted with and often on reasonably good terms with the children." The observers went on to describe the handling of hearings:

The judge spoke slowly, clearly, and explained each step of the process, its consequences and all decisions until the child and his parents said they understood. Parents, children, and all interested parties in the courtroom were asked to speak. The judge seemed to know the record quite thoroughly. And he explained, when appropriate, how to get the record erased, as well as the importance of getting a record erased.

Despite a generally positive description, the report continued, "in general, the children and their parents were submissive and reluctant to speak, and the lawyers seemed to play a very small role in this type of procedure."

In deciding what to do in a child's best interests, a juvenile court judge draws on a social investigation prepared by a probation officer. The report covers the youngster's background: family situation, school and social adjustment. Ideally, the resulting picture is of the "whole child," but the overall impression is that the courts too often lack such a picture. Time and manpower are lacking in the probation staffs. Chapter 6 will discuss the work of probation officers in detail.

Probation reports are designed to help the judge with disposition of the case, they are not intended to be used when the facts of a case are decided. In an adult criminal case, past record or background is usually inadmissible in adjudicating the present charge. Not necessarily so with children. In recent years, court reformers have criticized the tendency for juvenile court judges to be influenced by a child's background in deciding the facts of the case. Here, too, progress was found. Among courts where information was gathered when probation officers conducted social investigations, two-thirds did not prepare such reports until after adjudication.

For the disturbingly large number of status offenders brought to juvenile court, the judge faces in acute form not only the problems of the child, but those of parents and, in the background, the problems of the community. Chief Judge David L. Bazelon of the District of Columbia has described what NCJW observers felt strongly in their own observations of what happens to status offenders in juvenile courts throughout the country:

First of all, immature and authoritarian parents use the court's jurisdiction as a threat to hang over their children, a way to get out of their own obligation to work with their children and even to "get their own way" in a specific conflict with their children. The tired and apathetic ones readily abdicate their parental roles, simultaneously relieved and lulled by the promise that the problem can be handled by the juvenile court.

Frequently, when a child runs away from home and is picked up by the police, his parents refuse to take him home, instead filing a beyond control complaint. In such cases the child may be held weeks or months pending hearing on the complaint. During this period of detention when he is held in close quarters with law violators the child may indeed acquire the ingrained attitudes of a true delinquent.

If the court cannot bring the child and parents together, the child is usually sent to the same training schools and institutions as a hardened offender until he is old enough to make his own way in the world. Small wonder that many of them openly avow that they might as well be hanged for a sheep as a lamb, and reappear shortly after release in the same court as bona fide delinquents. If we somehow managed to make our juvenile courts more efficient, we might only succeed in cranking out juvenile delinquents more efficiently.*

The burden of Judge Bazelon's argument became a major concern of NCJW observers of juvenile courts throughout the country. The courts are getting cases that they cannot handle constructively, cases that do not belong there in the first place. Status offenders need to be diverted from the court system, not dumped into it.

Awareness of this needed change is spreading throughout the system of juvenile justice. NCJW observers report that court officials, from judges on down, cite the need for the community to face up to its responsibilities to provide resources outside the court system. Judge Bazelon pointed out that juvenile courts act in truancy, runaway and "incorrigible" cases on the premise that "if we don't act, no one else will." Instead, he says the opposite is true: because the courts act, "no one else does."

*Judge David L. Bazelon, "Beyond Control of the Juvenile Court," *Juvenile Court Journal,* vol. 21, no. 2, Summer 1970.

However, nationwide NCJW reports cite few examples of juvenile court judges responding to Judge Bazelon's admonition that it is up to them "to call attention" to the needs in justice for children. Judges, for the most part, are not taking an active part in arousing the community. There are exceptions. In two instances—in Erie County, Pennsylvania, and Tucson, Arizona—NCJW Sections spearheaded action programs in cooperation with juvenile court judges.

After Erie Section completed its study of juvenile justice, the findings were shared at an open meeting with representatives from concerned organizations. This led to formation of a steering committee embracing groups ranging from the League of Women Voters to the Drug Counseling Center. The aim was to develop community involvement, and the next step was to approach the county juvenile court judge, Fred Anthony. He responded enthusiastically and placed the power of his office behind their efforts, which centered particularly on developing alternatives to sending juveniles away to training institutions. The work went forward under a Resources for Youth group, whose members receive official appointment from Judge Anthony and who make recommendations on the constructive disposition of cases. "In nearly every instance the recommendations of the committee have been followed," an NCJW committee member reported, "and, to date, the court has been most satisfied with the suggestions made."

In Tucson, the NCJW Section formed a coalition to support the efforts of a new juvenile court judge. His progressive approach was in line with what the Section found in its community study. Support was rallied for Judge John P. Collins' campaign for better facilities, diversion of many cases, and higher salaries for juvenile court personnel so that the staff could be upgraded. After its first year, the coalition succeeded in pressuring county authorities into building three group homes and raising probation salaries. Judge Collins, who was conducting a vigorous effort of his own, responded from the beginning. As a NCJW participant reported, he was "delighted to have community support and promised any help we might need."

A notable sign of awareness outside the court system was a plank in the 1972 Democratic Party platform calling for "revision of the juvenile court system: dependency and neglect cases must be removed from the corrections system and clear distinctions must be drawn between petty childhood offenses and the more serious crimes." Earlier, the 1970 White House Conference on Children urged "a first step" toward improving the system of juvenile justice: "children's offenses that would not be crimes if committed by an adult—such as truancy, runaway, curfew violation, and incorrigibility—should not be processed through the court system, but diverted to community resources."

The problem, as underscored by the NCJW reports, is that status offenders are lumped together with serious delinquents in all phases of the system of juvenile justice, overloading its resources and facilities, and escalating youthful rebellion or maladjustment to criminal behavior. Moreover, as already noted, the system also punishes the innocent young whose crime is being born to troubled or irresponsible parents.

The heart of this misguided handling of juveniles is the legal fact that the juvenile court has wide jurisdiction. The vicious circle cannot be broken unless the jurisdiction is changed. Basically, that is why the NCJW Task Force, after studying the reports from its Sections, urged the de-criminalizing of "children's crimes." It recommended that *state laws be changed to exclude status offenders from the juvenile court and correctional systems*. As will become clear in reporting on the latter, damage done to juveniles in the process from arrest through detention and courtroom is compounded in correctional systems.

5 Putting Children Away

In a training school for eight-to-fourteen-year-olds, the director looked out over rolling green acres and spoke for the children in his charge: "No matter how beautiful the training school and no matter how horrible the conditions at home, most of the children still want to go home. That's all they have in the world."

Such as Timothy M., whose situation was cited in another context by a former legal aid attorney. His mother refused to let him come home on visits from his training school, much less come home on parole. Timothy could not believe this was true. The training school felt that he should remain in custody because he "avoids reality."

The lesson is of power and powerlessness. The power of the juvenile justice system as exercised by the courts and as expressed by the institutions to which courts commit children. The powerlessness of children who lose their freedom as members of what the National Juvenile Law Center called in 1970 "the most discriminated-against class in the world."

Training schools, camps, reception and diagnostic centers—separate and distinct from detention centers—incarcerated an increasing number of children during the 1960's. While the population of adults in prison was declining, the number of children in correctional institutions was increasing.

In 1971 an official census of juvenile correctional facilities showed admissions and discharges each at about 85,000 a year, with an average daily population of 35,931 in training schools; 5,666 in ranches, forestry camps and farms; and 1,045 in halfway houses and group homes. (An additional 2,486 were in reception or diagnostic centers.) Of the 85,000 admissions that year, over 50,000 were first commitments.*

After observers from the National Council of Jewish Women visited 50 training schools in every part of the country, and collected data about them, their resulting reports flowed in two directions: 1) what training schools are like, and how they operate; and 2) whether or not they should continue to exist. What observers found ranged from laudatory efforts to callous jail-keeping. In any case, training schools were escaping community attention or concern.

When observers talked to staff members at training schools, the comments often followed a common theme: "We try *not* to hurt the kids while they are here." Or as expressed by the superintendent of a New England training school: he thought that boys probably didn't go out any worse than they came in. Instead of successful rehabilitation, observers found holding operations—with exceptions at both extremes, of promising programs and flagrant failures.

Once committed, an alarming number of children are committed again and again, returning as damning witnesses to the failure to rehabilitate. The

*Children in Custody, A Report on the Juvenile Detention and Correctional Facility Census of 1971, U.S. Department of Justice, Law Enforcement Assistance Administration, National Criminal Justice and Statistics Service.

training in training schools too often is chiefly in crime, as one West Coast teenager said in labeling her training school "stupid": "In there you learn more than when you went in. That is bad. If you're mature enough, you don't do that. But otherwise you might listen and get in more trouble."

This is borne out by the rates on recidivism. One professional in rehabilitation even cited the need to meet youngsters as soon as they get off the bus on being released: "Many get into trouble right away and many of the girls get pregnant immediately." More than two-fifths of the training schools observed by NCJW reported recidivism that was over 45 percent or described as "very high." Nationally, recidivism in juvenile institutions has been estimated as even higher, ranging from 50 to 80 percent. In his talk before the Baltimore Section of NCJW, Senator Birch Bayh indicted incarceration as "the most costly means of dealing with juvenile offenders, both in monetary terms and in terms of the cost to society of making hardened criminals from first offenders." He cited "a remarkable 70 percent recidivism rate for institutionalized first offenders." The longer-range implications were brought home to one NCJW Section in the South on learning that 65 to 75 percent of the 2,200 inmates in the state's federal penitentiary are products of juvenile institutions.

What happens to children committed to institutions was evident from first-hand observation. Several NCJW reports cited particular problems for incarcerated girls. These begin upon entry, when many institutions routinely require an internal examination. As one report from the East noted, this was done "regardless of age. They hastened to say that most of the girls were accepting and that no one was forced but that all were required to have one. I can only hope that in the case of a first-time examination there is kindness and understanding."

The fact is that many girls wind up in institutions for "sexual offenses." Reporting on their visit to a girls' training school, a Midwest Section wrote: "Girls usually committed are charged with running away, incorrigibility, truancy and sex offenses. . . . Sex offenses usually are pre-marital relations, not criminal sex offenses."

One result is the incarceration of pregnant girls. Superintendents of training schools candidly admitted that their lack of appropriate facilities and services made such commitments highly undesirable.

The overwhelming reality for children in training schools is that their freedom is taken away and they are confined to institutions that usually are too large and too far away. In the typical rural settings for training schools, children find themselves a long way from home. The distance is not only a source of personal pain but a major obstacle to any rehabilitation program. In only eight percent of the communities in the NCJW study were training schools within 20 miles of children's homes. Three times that proportion were more than 150 miles away, including a few that were more than 400 miles away. About half were between 51 and 150 miles away. These findings reflect in-state placements. The sporadic pattern of out-of-state placements carries the problem to its extreme.

NCJW reports cited a number of problems stemming from the distant locations of training schools. Children of all ages who have been uprooted and committed to institutions, many of them away from home and neighborhood for the first time, are effectively cut off from their families. It takes time, money, and logistics for families to visit training schools, which are usually in areas with limited public transportation services. Visiting schedules are usually rigidly limited to weekends. While several training schools provide buses to transport parents, these are the exceptions. The result is a heavy burden upon the families, which are usually poor and least able to afford—or arrange—visiting trips. The result for the child is further isolation and an extra measure of psychological pain.

An example is the case of Jose C., a fourteen-year-old boy who, during almost a year in a training school, had not received a visit from his mother. An NCJW observer investigated further and found that the mother, who spoke no English, did not know where he was (he had been transferred from one institution to another). The trip, which involved a two-hour bus ride and a taxi to the school, was $21—a cost which her welfare allotment did not cover.

Isolation and distance make it impossible for training school staff to work with the child's family, which often needs help as much or more than the child. (In a few cases, notably in California, training schools arrange family sessions during weekend visits.) Out in the country, the staff cannot coordinate its efforts with a child's local community resources which could help while the child is committed, and afterwards. The result is that one group of professionals concerned with the child's rehabilitation in placement has little or no contact with the crucial family and neighborhood setting. The other group—facing the child after release—comes on cold, without any contact during the training school experience. A child, already troubled and in trouble, comes and goes as a stranger from one arena of professional help to another.

Typically urban, the children in training schools end up in an environment that looks lovely on postcards and in official brochures. But it bears no resemblance to the urban world from which they came and to whose harsh realities they must return. In one training school, an "ombudsman" assigned to monitor children's rights, summed up the dilemma of rural training schools: "These kids learn to make it with the trees, but this doesn't help them when it's time to go home."

If distance breeds isolation from reality, size of training schools generates impersonality. The more children the less time for personal attention and the more overworked the staff; the larger the institution the more need for regimentation, the less chance for rehabilitation. It is a problem that was singled out by the 1970 White House Conference on Children, which recommended elimination of all large institutions as soon as possible. No more than 100 youngsters should be housed in existing institutions; actually, few children should be housed in facilities holding more than 20.

At the time of the White House Conference recommendation, the National Center for Social Statistics reported on the basis of 325 institutions responding that over half had more than 100 children. The NCJW reports on training schools underlined this problem. More than half (56 percent) had over 100 children; one-fifth had more than 200. Observers found one training school with 757 children. The Justice Department's 1971 census found that 75 percent of the country's training schools had a capacity of over 100 children.

Testifying against a proposal to construct a large institution in Maryland, NCJW stated:

Yearly institutional costs per child are currently $12,000. It can be no less in a new maximum security facility and, in fact, will undoubtedly grow larger. Once the building is there, the state will be committed to an annual minimum outlay of $1,200,000 and there will no longer be any choice. That money can buy a great deal of the kind of attention and therapy which, given to children in their own homes or even in foster care or group homes, can help them adjust to society instead of following the same course, taken by too many today, from minor offense to hardened adult (or even juvenile) criminal.

In visits to training schools, what met the eye revealed a great deal. The physical setup reflected the approach toward incarceration; the facilities indicated the kind of life children were forced to lead. The staffs did not hide their own feelings on the problems, either, repeatedly calling attention to them. Typically, at a Midwest training school, the staff was found to be "anxious to inform our interviewers about the conditions and problems of the school" and "seemed to feel that only through education of the public could changes be brought about at the school."

In that school, as in others visited, the realities of custody and the inadequacy of facilities were on full and obvious view: "The facilities are poor, out-of-date, in need of repair, even new facilities seemed to be inadequate (size of rooms, bathrooms, etc.). Recreational facilities exceptionally poor—dirty unsanitary pool, no filter, toilets unclean. No private toilets, no partitions. No bars on windows, but heavy restraining devices. Doors are kept locked."

At a training school in the East where it costs more than $12,000 a year per child: "The general physical impression was one of quiet, of cleanliness, but of drabness. The boys are housed in a two-story building in five wings or cell blocks euphemistically called 'cottages.' Each boy has a tiny cubicle furnished with bed, desk and chair. He is permitted to hang pictures and clippings. He may not enter another's room; this is an attempt to limit homosexual encounters. The room doors, with barred windows, are locked at 10 p.m., any child wishing to use the bathroom afterwards must call and bang on his door for release."

At a Midwest boys training school, observers were confronted "by a sentry house at the main gate, where we signed in, plus a ten-foot-high chain link fence with barbed wire along the top. . . . The talk-in entrance gate was unlocked at all times, but it obviously was in view of the sentry house." It is considered a "medium security school."

At first sight, a center for boys in the South, "a single large building of contemporary design," looked like "an impregnable fortress." Once inside, the impression was less formidable; the center appeared to be a model example. A further look revealed that the center had no gym facilities, no provision for vocational training, and a lack of trained and qualified personnel.

In a Midwest training school populated by boys committed mainly for theft or running away, observers tried to piece together the various elements of life at the institution. Their account reflects the uneven picture which tended to emerge in reports on training schools. What they do or how they operate does not indicate a pattern of atrocities, neither does it indicate successful rehabilitation. Like so many training schools, this one belongs somewhere between fulsome praise and unmitigated blame. The school was trying, but its efforts prompt the query: To what avail?

A staff of 45 handles a capacity population of 135 in an "open institution with excellent school, recreational and treatment facilities" and with a locked security section for boys "who have or may run away." Next the details: "The privacy at this institution is extremely limited. The boys live in large dormitories but can win, as a special privilege for good behavior, private sleeping quarters in a partitioned section. The boys are given a good deal of responsibility and decision-making within clearly-defined limits. Some visit home frequently. The facility is basically well-run with a good program and an involved staff. However, the dormitories in which the boys sleep were in extremely poor condition. Paint was peeling off the walls, the mattresses were falling apart, and the rooms were dismal and depressing. Better physical conditions would greatly help the morale of the boys. The recidivism rate runs very high, about 50 percent. The staff is concerned about the lack of community support, and a generally negative view of all institutions makes it more difficult for the staff to help the boys face their responsibilities. It has also been many years since the juvenile judge visited this institution."

Putting Children Away

Scattered throughout first-hand reports are individual comments that reveal self-defeating lapses in training school operations . . . "educational growth is stressed; however no place did we see books for the boys to enjoy at their leisure" . . . "saw only about one-fifth of kids actually in classrooms, irrelevant and outdated textbooks; a refrigerator in every cottage—empty" . . . "These children are the forgotten children of the state. In 1971 all they received was a bar of soap for Christmas. Thanks to Council, in 1972 they were remembered" . . . "At the state training school for boys, decent food is being ruined and rendered unpalatable because the state will not pay for a cook who could properly prepare this food."

A glimpse of life in a more favorable training school emerged from an observation visit by an NCJW Section on the East Coast.

We arrived to see the buildings scattered over hills on many acres of ground in a rather lovely country setting. Immediately we were impressed by the lack of fences or barred windows. . . . Children in need of supervision, not delinquents, enter through the Juvenile Courts. There is no orientation or reception unit. On the day of arrival children are given a complete physical examination and achievement tests, and grouped accordingly. There are nine living units with 20-22 boys in each dormitory. Capacity of the institution is 170. The units are staffed with a seven-man team with 24-hour coverage and double coverage at peak hours. They have a youth center program, "helping through caring." They have peer-group therapy with boys meeting four times a week for 1½-hour sessions with a group leader and no more than 10 boys at a time. They attend school five days a week 12 months a year. There are 3 vocational units and 6 academic. They have 22 full-time teachers.

The boys wear their own clothes and may have personal objects in their rooms. Welfare provides clothes for needy children. The boys have their own bank account and can earn money in the work release program or can earn points for achievement in school to spend in the canteen.

The boys are taken on trips, recreational and cultural. They use parks in the vicinity for camping, go bowling, swimming, to movies and dances. They seem to try to give them as many opportunities as possible in normal outside situations. Their day:
6:45 Wash, dress and eat
8:05 School
12:00 Lunch, then back to school
3:30-4:30 Trips or planned program
5:00 Dinner
5:30 Back to unit for group sessions or recreation

We visited one unit and were favorably impressed. Six units are new and the 20-22 boys have private rooms plus a group bathroom, a TV room, and a recreation room with a ping-pong table and pool table. We were fortunate in being able to speak to one of the boys alone. We truly received a good report.

The staff felt as though more community education and involvement would help tremendously in giving the boys personal contact and a sometime home environment which an institution cannot provide. Money is always needed to provide the extras.

Our impression was a good one. There appeared to be an informal atmosphere, well-kept facilities, and people who cared.*

---

*NCJW observers reacted favorably to this insitution as compared to other institutions. But two questions come to mind: 1) is not a rural insitutional setting socially debilitating for the child who must ultimately "make it" in the community; and 2) what is the justification for incarcerating children who have committed no crime, even in a "good" training school.

Putting Children Away

Training school staffs use a stick-and-carrot approach to keep children in line. Children live between the threat of solitary confinement and the promise of special privileges and rewards. Their experience in the system of juvenile justice maintains its consistency: power belongs to adult authority.

Solitary confinement has its euphemisms: "meditation cottages," "intensive treatment units," "room confinement." A youngster is confined alone to a room, which, in one training school, earned the invidious label, "coffin box." A *New York Times* reporter describes his visit to such a room, which was empty except for a crumbling foam-rubber mattress on a built-in platform. The inmate, a girl who said she would be "sweet sixteen" in a few days, had two ways of looking out—through a small window in the locked door at the empty corridor or through a screened window at an empty volleyball court.

Judging from the nationwide NCJW reports, solitary confinement is widely used in training schools, ranging from a few hours to a few days. In some schools, youngsters are confined to their own rooms during the day; in others, they are sent to the "treatment center" or "corrections building" for solitary confinement. In one Midwest school, observers found that the door was left open for a youngster with claustrophobia, but he was chained to the bed.

One training school in the South applies a "special program" to a rule-violator. He is transferred to a locked building and kept there until his rebellious behavior ends. This can last from a few hours to a few weeks, with the youngster confined to a sparsely furnished room and deprived of free movement. He is let out for cleaning details and for exercise in the yard. Where the stay becomes extended, teachers come by with school work.

In general, solitary confinement is regarded as a last resort and its use is usually restricted. However, the practice is within staff discretion subject to administrative approval. The trend is to require an explanation for the decision to isolate a youngster and to limit the length of isolation. The staff is expected to stay in touch with an isolated youngster and not to abandon him or her. In New York, after the Legal Aid Society sued on behalf of a fourteen-year-old girl held in isolation for 13 days, a federal injunction was issued against extended isolation. Subsequently, the New York State Division for Youth imposed a 24-hour limit on solitary confinement and banned its use either for treatment or punishment, limiting its use "only in cases where a child constitutes a serious danger to himself and others." Such regulation of the use of solitary is necessary; its implementation, however, requires monitoring. Further, there is a basic question as to whether solitary confinement should be used at all.

Other "last resort" methods for dealing with youngsters include corporal punishment. In one school, where only the director may administer such punishment, he described the effect as only temporary and effective particularly with the younger children. In some instances, it was learned that "hard-core" troublemakers are transferred to adult prisons.

To a certain extent, drugs are used to control children in training schools, with indications that they are used more for girls than boys. Only a handful of NCJW reports said that tranquilizers or similar medication are issued routinely, but almost two-fifths of those reporting said it was used on "some" children. More than half of the reports said such medication is not used routinely, though several noted that this was a recent change of policy.

Various examples were found of what was called behavior modification. The examples ranged from a monthly reward of $1 at the canteen and a gain of one week toward early release for the outstanding boy and girl in a cottage, to a ranking system. In the latter, a youngster remains a freshman for his first month, advancing to sophomore for satisfactory behavior and gaining such privileges as going to a ball game, a concert, or a movie. In another month, he can become a junior which means one-day passes. Finally, on becoming a senior, he receives weekend passes to go home and various other privileges, each step part of the preparation for leaving the training school altogether. In an eastern training school where a ranking system is used, the boys participate in evaluating and placing each other on the levels.

Teenagers underscored what they really want in conversations with observers. They want contact with adults who care and who listen.

The worst thing (about being in an institution) is that your feelings are locked up. Everything that goes on— school, arts, crafts, etc.—is nothing if you can't get your feelings out. . . . If there was a place kids knew they could go for help they would go. I don't mean jail. I mean where they know they could talk with someone who would listen.

Training schools in various parts of the country are building in that listening process with group therapy and rap sessions. In Florida, NCJW observers were particularly impressed with Group Guided Interaction, a method based on the reality therapy of psychiatrist William Glasser. At one training school, it was singled out as "the most important happening." In daily sessions with their counselors, the boys thrash out their problems and work on ways to "make it" on the outside. The focus is on coping with present problems rather than seeking their origins in the past. Instead of the question, "Did you do right or wrong?", the question posed is, "Did you do it responsibly—meeting your needs while respecting the needs of others?" Observers report, "Peer pressures become a dynamic force in influencing students to accept responsibility for the behavior of others with whom they participate in treatment."

The program's expressed goals evolve toward rehabilitation:

Identify individual problems

Work on solving problems

Overcome sitting on problems

To help each other to go home

To make it at home.

Irrespective of the setting, children stay too long in the institutions observed in the NCJW study. Many reports described the average length of stay as "indefinite," emphasizing the powerlessness of children subject to adult discretion. One observer, commenting on how children's behavior is judged, asked pointedly, "Is the kid better or just playing the game better?" As it is, of 50 training schools observed, the average stay was more than seven months in 60 percent of them, more than 10 months in 36 percent.

Keeping youngsters in training schools—particularly those that are too large and too far away—succeeds . . . in keeping them away. An insidious process overtakes the children. They become "institutionalized." They tend to take on an "inmate personality." As one teenager complained, "We feel like robots—we are programmed." The longer they remain the more likely they are to emphasize adjustment to the institution than to the outside world they must eventually re-enter.

In a discussion with the NCJW Task Force, Sister Mary Paul of a New York City diagnostic center, cited "the quantity of deprivation" imposed upon an institutionalized child. Not all the elements of deprivation are found in all training schools, but the common theme of institutionalization is generally present. A child is uprooted, taken from family and friends, stripped of familiar emotional and psychological supports and forced to submit to a totally different world run largely as they see fit by the adults in authority. (In one training school, for some unexplained reason, all children were required to take two showers a day. In another, the boys go freely in groups to the nearby community for bowling and movies, but when taken to the community hospital for X-rays or surgery, they are handcuffed.) Often clothing is taken away and the youngster is forced to wear a uniform. (In two institutions visited, NCJW teams observed all the children in stocking feet. Asked about this, the administrators said they could "not afford to buy shoes for every child.") Possessions are kept by institution officials, and in dormitories there is scanty personal space. The child lives with little or no privacy, and close personal relationships are viewed with suspicion. Mail is opened and censored. (One superintendent of a women's facility asked a meeting of corrections officials: "Why open the mail? Is it worth the time? How much important information have we gotten over the years?")

Typically, the institutionalized child depends on the adult counselor or supervisor for basic human needs, ranging from a bar of soap to warmth, attention. (Said one teenager: "If you're lucky, you get houseparents who understand . . .") This can lead to psychological exploitation of the children who live in a state of organized dependence. All around, they must cope with a pecking order of power, which leaves youngsters at the bottom. Unless a healthy atmosphere is maintained, they, in turn, struggle for limited areas of supremacy in a child-fight-child atmosphere. With the exception of progressive training schools, the child is deprived of the smallest opportunity for personal decision-making—the very capacity that increases the likelihood of making it on the outside. Instead, he is conditioned to submitting, to conformity, to obedience under pressure, to surrendering the very urge toward self-assertion that reached out for expression when he got into trouble. (Observers reported that in one training school, "the boys learn job skills, but not enough to get jobs if any were available . . . the main thrust of the vocational education is how to work and to accept authority.")

The former counsel for the National Council on Crime and Delinquency, Sol Rubin, has written of children as "victims of institutionalization." He underscored the need to break down the system of deprivation surrounding the institutionalized child: "to attack the means by which the child is held to being a non-person, to restore autonomy to him, to grant him what is truly needed, not to impose conformity on him and destroy his growth and independence."* Milton Luger, Director of the New York State Division for Youth, pointed in the same direction when he discussed training schools before the 19th annual conference of the National Institute on Crime and Delinquency in June 1972. "Our orientation," he said, "more and more will be towards the community rather than towards building programs on campus. We have got to mix these youths in with the real world with which they must learn to cope, rather than with institutional activities to which they have been encouraged to adjust."

While a many-sided picture was pieced together from observations of training schools around the country, one consistent point of view did emerge. While the reports varied on what training schools are in the concrete and what they are like in various states, they led to a consensus view that training schools should be phased out. This became the recommendation of the NCJW Task Force on Justice for Children: *that there be no further construction of large training schools; those existing should be closed.*

It is not so much that training schools are all bad, but that they have not proved to be an effective method of rehabilitation. The Task Force reasoned from the stated goal of juvenile justice systems throughout

---

*Sol Rubin, "Children as Victims of Institutionalization," *Child Welfare,* vol. LI, no. 1, 1972.

the country: rehabilitation, not punishment. Given this goal, community, educational and treatment services are matters of right not privilege for children in institutions. When they are deprived of rehabilitation—as well as the education and medical attention due all children—then incarceration itself may violate the law. But the aim of the NCJW study was not accusatory; it was to change children from victims to beneficiaries of the system of juvenile justice.

The State of Massachusetts has already led the way in closing large institutions for children. In 1969, Jerome Miller, then Commissioner of the Youth Services Department, announced that the state was getting out of the business of "warehousing" children. In 1972, Massachusetts became the first state to close all juvenile institutions, "a basic decision" reflecting considerations cited by Dr. Miller: "that it would do no good to pump more money and more programs into the existing system because the system can chew up reforms faster than you can dream up new ones." He called it "a sick system that destroys the best efforts of everyone in it and we decided to look for alternatives."

The Massachusetts juvenile system, which had been like the others throughout the country, was not working. Recidivism was running between 60 and 80 percent, instances of brutality were found throughout the system, and a substantial amount of money was being spent to maintain failure, $11,000 to $12,000 a year per child—"enough," in Dr. Miller's estimate, "to send a child to Harvard with a $100-a-week allowance, a summer vacation in Europe, and once-a-week psychotherapy."

In Massachusetts, group homes were established, foster-home placements expanded, a stay-at-home program established in conjunction with special treatment services. Closed facilities were set up for the small number (an estimated 70 out of 1200) who needed them. Even here, intensive care and therapy were planned, with the goal of sending these children home.

When the Worcester Section of NCJW looked into the Massachusetts program, Dr. Miller had left to direct juvenile corrections in Illinois, and the system in Massachusetts was under pressure and criticism. The policy of opening community-based homes was bogged down in financing problems and in community opposition. Calling community support a major problem, the Worcester Section described the opposition as "vociferous"—it was touching the raw nerve of community willingness to respond to the problem. "The shock of de-institutionalization," the Section reported, "has forced the court systems and social agencies to think through the disposition of juvenile cases far more carefully than when youngsters could simply be committed to a training school."

A regional director of the Department of Youth Services put the problem in a perspective shared by other NCJW Sections around the country. Singling out a scapegoat in the system of juvenile justice avoids the larger issue. "If DYS is really in a state of confusion," he said, "then it is not entirely because of its own internal problems. It owes some of the blame to schools, court and probation staffs, police, private social agencies, mental health, and indeed, entire communities, because of their failure and unwillingness to support even their own problem children."

When NCJW canvassed its Sections throughout the country, group homes emerged as a priority area for action. The focus was placed on a small residence program where five to 12 youngsters live in a home-like atmosphere, go to school in the neighborhood and draw on community resources.

The reactions of NCJW observers were typified in an optimistic report after visiting both training schools and group homes in the Midwest. While allowing for the fact that the group homes visited only accept children they think they can help, the observers stated: "We left the group homes with a hopeful feeling for the future of their inhabitants. The minimum security atmosphere and the ability to attend community schools certainly helped to make the youngsters feel that they could work out solutions to their problems. The professional staffs at both group homes were genuinely interested in the children and seemed to achieve a high degree of success as far as rehabilitation was concerned."

Group homes are not a cure-all, as the NCJW Task Force realistically advised: "It is vitally important that group homes be used only for the small proportion of children who *really* need to live away from home." Foster home placement or living with understanding relatives are other alternatives in the same line, each to be considered according to the child's individual needs. Above all, there is the overriding reality that only about ten percent of the children brought to court need to be taken away from their families. Most children belong where they want to be—with their own families. And most often, this is achieved through probation.

6 On Probation

In the twilight zone of probation, a child's world is defined by the terms and conditions set forth by juvenile court. On the one hand, as outlined in a western state, the official papers remind the child of the helping hand: "You will be under supervision of a probation counselor during the period of probation. He or she will be available to help you with any problems you may have. Do not hesitate to call your probation counselor if you are in doubt or in trouble." On the other hand, "if the probationer violates any of the terms and conditions," a court hearing can change, extend, or revoke probation. The choice is the prescribed help or the consequences.

The general "terms and conditions," typical of the probationary systems throughout the country, are:

1. Not to violate any laws.

2. Obey your parents, legal guardians or custodians, probation counselors, and school officials.

3. If enrolled in school, attend regularly unless validly

excused. If not, get a job or enroll in a job-training program.

4. Keep your appointments with your probation counselor and follow his instructions. Advise your probation counselor within 48 hours of any change of address or telephone number.

5. Be at home at the hours agreed upon by your parents, legal guardians or custodians, and your probation counselor.

6. Obey the court's orders.

7. If placed with an individual or agency, obey the rules and regulations.

After any "special conditions" of the probation are added, the form is signed by the judge, the youngster, parent or guardian, and probation counselor. The shadow of the system of juvenile justice thereby falls upon the individual child, who is neither in custody nor fully free, but accountable to a probation officer, who once again confronts the child with discretionary power vested in adult authority.

Probation, at once the most promising, the most popular, and the most fragile alternative in the system of juvenile justice, places heavy responsibilities upon the individual officer. His social-psychological territory as mapped in one expert summary includes the following: The probation officer "must understand the motivations of human behavior, the influence of physical, mental and emotional health on conduct and family relationships. He must be informed as to community problems and their effects on individual attitudes and patterns."*

As the eyes and ears of the system of juvenile justice, the probation officer is surrounded by the system's well-meaning intentions and its frustrating lapses,

---

*John P. Kenney and Dan G. Pursuit, *Police Work With Juveniles* (Springfield, Mass.: Charles C. Thomas, 10959), p. 276.

its wide-gauge responsibilities and narrow-gauge resources, and all the detours and dead ends of its operations. Perhaps more than anyone else in the system of
juvenile justice, the probation officer experiences its am-
biguities and its limitations.

While the most important work of probation officers is to help and supervise youngsters in trouble, they
are involved in all parts of the system. This involvement
includes intake and investigation as well as supervision.
Intake, as previously described in chapter 2 on *The Gatekeepers*, covers screening of each case to decide whether
juvenile court should step in or whether the case should
be diverted. In a middle ground between diverting a
case entirely and filing a court petition, the probation officer may place a child on "informal probation"—this side
of court action and therefore unofficial, but leaving the
officer free to send the child to court if he eventually
sees fit. This often occurs without consulting anyone. At
times, children have been committed to institutions without appearing before a judge.

In preparing social investigations, the probation
officer influences the way the judge handles a case after
making his decision on the facts. Sometimes, as noted in
chapter 4, *Children in Court*, judges also consult these
reports in the adjudicatory or fact-finding phase of court
action. This practice has been denounced by reformers
and was found, in the NCJW study, to be on the decline.
(However, it was noted that the very existence of a
folder on a child can prejudice the judge's decision at adjudication.)

To carry on a social investigation, the probation
officer needs the time to visit neighborhood and home, to
interview family, relatives, and friends. Often, they are
not accessible, and often the neighborhood itself presents
a problem, as one NCJW Section noted: "While the officer should of course visit the child's home and neighborhood, probation officers are people like the rest of us, and
are rightfully fearful of venturing into reputedly unsafe

or hostile neighborhoods. It is understandable that their reports may be less than complete. And yet it is these reports, transmitted to the court through a liaison probation officer, that contain the suggestions for disposition that the judge reads and, in many cases, acts upon."

When a judge does decide to draw on the increasingly widespread alternative of probation, the centripetal-centrifugal forces of probationary supervision come into play. The officer is supposed to be a friend of the child and an officer of the court at the same time. The child is supposed to come to him with his troubles, while the probation officer has the responsibility of turning in the child for misconduct. The terms and conditions of probation are policed by the probation officer.

On the West Coast, a state attorney general's office provided an official inventory of the probation officer's two roles of court officer and social worker. (However, juvenile justice expert Lois Forer, who calls the functions of a juvenile probation officer "incompatible," would not agree with the heading which reads, "No Conflict Between Functions".)

The separation is described as follows:

Court Officer (arm of the court)

A creature of the statute and must work only within those limitations. Only an *agent* of the court with no authority to change orders of the court, or to disregard them.

He carries out all orders of the court.

He makes investigations and determines whether a child should come before the court by filing a petition.

He makes factual objective reports to the court so that the court may make a wise decision.

He makes suggestions and recommendations to the court.

He keeps the court informed as to progress made with court wards.

He is the legal representative of the juvenile court.

Statute provides no order or modification may be made by the juvenile court judge unless notice is given to the probation officer by the judge or clerk.

Social Worker

He conducts a social investigation, subjective analysis, works out a realistic plan for each case he presents to court.

No child should be placed on probation without a specific plan formulated in advance.

On a casework basis he supervises and gives consultation and guidance to both ward and his family. There is little point in granting probation unless a plan is prepared and adequate casework supervision is continued until the child no longer needs such.

Based on 66 reports covering probation around the country, the NCJW Task Force found adequate supervision a major obstacle in implementing probation successfully. Here are the main points drawn from the report:

The caseload of probation officers is on the average too high.

Too much is asked of probation staffs that are too small.

Low salaries make it difficult to recruit and keep qualified personnel.

Continuity is often lacking in handling a child.

Many probation departments lack procedural guidelines.

Encouraging signs: volunteer involvement in probation

On Probation

programs is beginning to spread, more so than anticipated, and innovations are being successfully tried.

Throughout the country, NCJW observers and probation officers reflected concern and complaints about caseloads. "My caseload numbers 120 active cases. I should see each case once a week, but because of the size of my caseload I see them once every two weeks or once a month." (Southwest) "Since the probation officer has an average of seven new investigations for the court per month and an ongoing caseload of thirty cases per month, this leaves even the most dextrous of probation officers with little time per case." (East Coast) "In the area of probation, the problem is numbers. There are not enough probation officers to go around." (South) "We have a lot of dedicated people giving over and above what is expected of them, but our caseloads are so high that we can only give token supervision. We're just trying to keep the lid down." (East) "Probation officers are carrying an unbearable load, covering intake, probation reports to the judge, family emergency counseling, visitations with the wards while detained, and attempts at after-care after release. All this and more while carrying a caseload more than double their capacity. More probation officers are needed. Probation officers must have smaller groups to handle, with more facilities to assist them." (West Coast)

The findings and comments dramatize data reported earlier by the President's Task Force on Juvenile Delinquency and Youth Crime. In 1966, 37 percent of probation officers in cities with a population of more than 100,000 saw children on their caseload once a month or less. Some saw them as infrequently as once every three months or less. While still connected with New York City's prison system, George F. McGrath, a well-known figure in his field, said of such a situation: "You don't really have probation when the officer is stuck with caseloads of 50 or 60 or 70 or a hundred kids. All you can do is paperwork. You're not counseling: you're not getting kids back to school; you're not getting them jobs."*

The 1966 data added details. At that time, about a quarter of a million children (223,800) were on probation for periods ranging from three to 36 months at a cost of $75.9 million. The report added: "Notwithstanding the size of that figure, salaries are low and caseloads high." A survey of 235 probation agencies found that the median salary was between $5,000 and $6,000. Caseloads averaged between 71 and 80 supervision cases, excluding social studies that took "at least half the time of most probation officers." Almost 11 percent of the children were in caseloads of more than 100.

Meanwhile, individual probation officers face the task at hand as best they can. Such as Mary K., a soft-spoken woman with a B.A. in social science who is assigned to the suburbs of a large midwestern city. Her responsibilities are investigation and supervision. An investigation involves seven to ten hours of information-gathering from police officers, teachers, and family. Reports are dictated over the phone to a secretary and recommendations made to the judge who "in 99 percent of the cases" follows them. Mary supervises a caseload of children from five to seventeen years of age, whom she sees once a month during probation periods that last from six months to one and one half years. On planned visits to homes and schools, she offers guidance, but finds parents "only superficially cooperative." If the children are sent to an institution, she visits them weekly. She cites as her goal helping the children to become adjusted, and reports that only ten percent of the children get into trouble again and are referred back to her. She singles out parents as her biggest roadblock because "they resist facing and understanding their children's problems."

The predominant majority (three-fourths) of probation officers in departments visited by NCJW have

---

*Quoted by Howard James in *Children in Trouble*, p. 89.

college degrees, with a master's degree required in some communities for a supervisory position. However, several communities reported problems in retaining staff. This was reflected in a probation officer's comment that "the job attracts many recent college graduates because it enables them to receive a weekly income while they read the want ads looking for a more permanent, better-paying job."

Where such an attitude prevails, a probation staff is certain to be afflicted with high turnover. This was detailed in an eastern community where in one of the three probation offices half the staff had been on the job less than six months. This was attributed to the low salary scale ($8,700 starting salary and $11,000 for supervisors) and to lack of opportunity for advancement. A previous policy of providing financial aid or time off for study was discontinued.

A promising sign is the increased use of in-service training. Almost two-thirds of the probation departments visited participate in some form of such training. Some communities go further, as in one where the detention center runs a series of in-service training programs and funds are provided for probation officers to attend training seminars in other parts of the country. While not definitive, this may reflect an improvement over the 1966 situation as reported by the President's Task Force on Juvenile Delinquency and Youth Crime. At that time, more than half (52 percent) in the sampling of probation departments reported that they had no in-service training program. Of those who had them only 21 percent met more often than once a month.

In his talk before the NCJW Joint Program Institute in January 1974, Congressman Tom Railsback singled out the task facing probation officers after pointing up the importance of specialized training for everyone involved in juvenile justice. "Probation officers especially are in need of help," he said. "The increasing concentration of young people in caseloads means far more work for these officers, because younger offenders tend to violate the conditions of their release more than others." Or as depicted by a probation officer speaking of his department: "Since juveniles need more attention than adults, the lack of manpower, funding and community placement are major difficulties."

Volunteers are helping to rescue the situation to such an extent that they are the rule rather than the exception. In more than two-thirds of the departments covered in NCJW reports, volunteers are involved in probation services, from intake to supervision. They have responded in particular to an appeal whose essence was expressed in an open letter from one judge to his juvenile court—"most of these youngsters can succeed on probation or supervision if they have an ongoing relationship with an individual they can trust—'someone who cares.' Someone they can look up to, respect—thus developing self-respect and positive goals." The judge asked the citizens (of Oakland County, Michigan) "to volunteer their time to work with youngsters as Case Aides."

This program, singled out as "magnificent" by the local NCJW Section, operates in five steps:

1. Volunteers contact the program for initial interview and filling out of applications.

2. After the initial interviews and screening of applications, orientation sessions are held.

3. A mutually agreeable case involving a child, or a family is matched with a selected volunteer.

4. A professional courtworker is assigned to the case and works closely with the volunteer.

5. The Case Aide Supervisor is always available as needed.

The main ingredients of this program parallel those of others found throughout the country: matching volunteer to youngster on a one-to-one basis and a direct tie-in with the professional probation worker assigned to the case.

A first-rate booklet designed to brief volunteers in the Oakland County, Michigan, Volunteer Case Aide Program, provides a summary of what is involved, while stressing the uniqueness of each and every case—"working with a youngster cannot be put in 'cookbook' form." The headings for the guidelines set forth the dimensions of counseling:

Keep in contact with the child

Patience

Be ready for setbacks

Give attention and affection

Be prepared to listen and to understand

Be a discerning listener

Don't pre-judge

Respect confidentiality, utterly and completely

Don't rush it, but as the relationship develops you can encourage the youngster to think about himself, his actions, goals, etc.

Report violations

Be supportive, encouraging, friendly, but also firm

Present your ideas clearly, firmly, simply. Always mean what you say and BE CONSISTENT. Be a good behavior model for the child. Avoid being caught in the middle

Positive reinforcement—praise and reward acceptable behavior

Such headings also indicate some of the quandaries inherent in the probation role, whether filled by staff or volunteer: the child's confidante and advocate is also the system's representative and monitor.

For volunteers who work with children, the satisfactions of the experience were spelled out in personal terms by members of an NCJW Section in the South. . . . "I'm so excited with the unending interest in this work with children I can't tell you. I put in approximately six to seven hours a week working with an assigned juvenile officer. My time is flexible, the staff marvelous. The color line is totally blurred. Kids are kids. I love it!" . . . "I look forward to visits with my cases. I feel really useful." . . . "I carry ten cases and have been working for two years. For me, the experience has been intense. I consider myself a 'professional.' Evaluation sessions with staff are available when I feel the need; by and large I can handle the work myself. I feel this to be most useful volunteering I've done." In sum, the Section reported over and over that excitement ran high with the women working through the juvenile court, and interest, with rare exceptions, increased with time.

Reports on volunteer programs also cited possible pitfalls in the reactions of professionals. Probation officers can feel that their jobs are threatened and that the work of volunteers reflects unfavorably on their own performance. In dealing with volunteers, some professionals may be inclined toward condescension. The result can be to give volunteers meaningless tasks, to ignore them and to drive them away. One NCJW Section, experienced in volunteer work, advised official support before getting underway; become involved "only after receiving a formal request from the judge of the juvenile court." This particular Section ran a two-year demonstration project for probation volunteers in which 25 to 30 volunteers served a minimum of three hours weekly. The volunteer probation project may be viewed as a community service with a built-in social reform component. It not only offers the opportunity for the probation department to involve the community and test the value of volunteer

On Probation

services, but it demonstrates in pilot form the advan-
tages of increased probation services as an alternative to
incarceration.

Another NCJW Section, which placed priority on
participating in its community Volunteer Probation Officer program, cited the program's success. Of 150 cases
covered, 65 youngsters had already been released from
probation and only one returned to court. That was on a
lesser charge more than a year after release. In seeking
more volunteers, the Section called attention to the en-
thusiastic observation by one of its members: "If there
was one dedicated volunteer for each 'Child Rated X,'
the sooner all would be rated 'G'."

NCJW Sections found recognition of the need to
go beyond symptoms and awareness of the underlying
problems that crowd in upon youngsters. One report
compared a child in trouble to a tire with a nail in it. No
matter how much air you add, there can be no solution
until the nail is removed and the hole patched. From one
probation worker's reflections on one youngster named
Louie, the larger context of probation can be sensed:

I don't think we're treating Louie's real problem. Louie's
real problem is that no one cares—neither his family nor
his community. Punish Louie for his offense, lock him up
in an institution and throw away the key. Out of sight,
out of mind. Don't bother to find out why he committed
the offense.

We just compound the problem. When the child
enters the court system he has a problem—when he
leaves he has two. He is now a juvenile delinquent. Until
we educate the families, and the community, our children
won't receive much help. Until we treat the entire
family—not punish the juvenile alone—we aren't giving
the child the help he needs. Do you know what Louie is?
Louie is the face of a statistic. There were 561 Louies on
probation in this county last year. There were 561 Louies

asking for help last year. Their chances were one in four of getting it.

In various cities, probation staffs were reaching out and getting closer to neighborhood and home. A highly praised example in the South involved a Community Based Casework Probation Service. Probation officers were reassigned from the central court building to strategically located offices in the heart of different sections of the city. More work was done with families. Thereafter, the rate of recidivism was cut in half—from 50 to 24 percent—and fewer younger siblings of delinquents were getting into trouble. When continued funding of this program was in jeopardy, NCJW and other community groups joined forces in a successful effort to obtain state support.

In another probation department, where NCJW observers were impressed with the "sincerity and dedication" of the staff and with the "flexibility" in the system, teamwork, specialization, and community-based operations were all in evidence. The three probation offices operated along slightly different lines, depending on the neighborhood served. The office handling the central city divided its probation officers into three groups. One group took cases through investigation and hearing; another picked up on supervision and treatment. This freed the latter probation officers from time-consuming investigation and also lifted the image of policeman-investigator, which inhibits interaction with youngsters. Still another group of probation officers visited the institutions; by specializing they made certain they could make regular visits.

A second probation office, operating out of a storefront office with a staff of five men and two women under a supervisor, used guided group interaction. Two probation officers were assigned to each group, which met twice a week. The supervisor reported that no one from the longest running group had become a repeater once probation ended. The office itself was open every day until 9 p.m. except on Friday, and officers were assigned to cases in pairs so one was always available as needed.

A third probation office was still in the process of moving completely from the central headquarters into the area being served. Investigation and supervision were already separated and group interaction was underway. The preliminary reports were already promising: the probation officers reported seeing the youngsters 50 percent more and recidivism showed signs of declining.

On the West Coast, a team of six probation officers was working with hard-core delinquents while they still were away at training camp. The officers, four of them with master's degrees, had a reduced caseload of 25 to 29 so that they could devote more time to the youngsters. After a youngster was released, five family group meetings were arranged for the first five weeks and psychiatric treatment provided as needed. The staff members had their own group meeting every other week with a consulting psychologist on hand to discuss the cases.

In a New England community, an intensive probation program was provided for youngsters 13 to 16 years old who came before juvenile court. During the program's first year, each teenager had seven major experiences while continuing to live at home: weekly counseling; family therapy sessions and parents' groups every other week; individual medical and dental examinations; bi-weekly "group-raps" for the teenagers; bi-weekly educational and vocational assistance; a weekly recreational program.

Participation in the 36-week program was a condition of probation. For the first 12 weeks, daily participation after school was required; for the second 12 weeks, on a weekly basis. The final 12 weeks involved evaluation leading to the decision on ending probation. After the first year, a study showed that 44 of the first 62 participants were kept out of institutions, including eleven who reappeared in court and were returned to the program. The cost comparison was also dramatic: $1,300 a year per youngster compared with $6,000 in a state training school.

Unfortunately, the Section report noted, the program reached only a limited number of youngsters as part of what was found to be an "exceptional" probation program. "The principal problem," the report added, "is that youngsters must be brought into the court system to benefit from these programs on any deeper level than referral to a community agency." This report, indicative of many, urged that similar, in-depth services be made available to all children and families—with the aim at prevention, not diversion.

With the aid of a state subsidy, a large West Coast probation department, which supervises 10,000 youngsters annually, reduced caseloads and kept more children out of institutions. Instead of the usual caseload of 65 to 70, the subsidized department dropped the number to 45 or less. Both the state and county benefitted, as did the child, who remained in his or her community and received intensive treatment. The state did not have to bear training school costs and the county was able to deal more effectively with children in trouble.

In viewing the role of the probation officer in the juvenile justice system, Judge Lois Forer has made pointed recommendations that in one way or another are evident in the foregoing innovations. Her recommendations also speak to the findings, reactions, and suggestions of NCJW Sections around the country. She urges that the probation officer be freed of an "ambivalent position" if he is "truly to be the key to rehabilitation" in working with youngsters: "If he is to help them, he cannot prosecute them. If he is to help them, he must have the resources with which to provide meaningful service." She recommends caseloads small enough so that each child can be seen at least once every two weeks and more often when desirable. There must be access to community resources that provide tutoring, recreation, medical care, employment, and whatever else a youngster needs in coping with his or her life situation. To be able to recognize a child's needs, the probation officer needs the proper mix of education, training and experience. This, in turn, calls for competitive salaries and the status the work deserves and requires.

More than anyone else, the probation officer is involved in the system in the beginning (intake), the middle (social investigation and recommendations) and the end (probation and "re-entry"). This constitutes a series of opportunities to make a difference in how the process operates, but only to a certain extent. Like all other professional components in juvenile justice, the probation officer is part of the system—which reflects and relies on the community.

Enter the National Council of Jewish Women. Nationwide study and involvement meant close contact with and working knowledge of the system. NCJW Sections are part of the community whose neglect and/or indifference toward juvenile justice is part of the problem. Being part of the problem makes it possible to be part of the solution—the action phase of Justice for Children. Some examples of this action have already been cited, but it is now time to delineate clearly two aspects of NCJW action:

HELPING HANDS—A report emphasizing the human dimensions of what is being done to overcome shortcomings, remove limitations, and improve the juvenile justice system.

REFORMS AND REMEDIES—An account of the campaign to change the system for the benefit of children and society at large.

Two roads toward one destination: Justice for Children.

7 Helping Hands

At a California detention center, an NCJW volunteer talked to a teenager named Ronnie about his feelings. He felt that the older generation didn't understand young people and was always putting them down with "Don't do this. Don't do that—They don't understand our desire to be free." The volunteer reminded Ronnie that she, too, had been young, had dreams, and wanted to "do my own thing." But, he countered, the older generation "doesn't care about us." When the volunteer answered that she cared, that was why she was there, Ronnie remarked, "But you are paid." When she explained that she was a volunteer, Ronnie blurted out: "You are? I never knew an old lady could be so sharp. . . . Not that I think you are old." Then by the volunteer's own report: "A few days later on a return visit I heard my name, 'Hi Perle.' Looking around I saw Ronnie. I felt good and warm inside. I had been accepted."

From Bridgeport, Conn., a Council member described the case of the "turned-off" youngster who was "turned-on" by guitar lessons. "It was a thrill to see her transformed from a withdrawn, lethargic girl into quite a bubbly, animated youngster."

Letter to a volunteer teacher from a 15-year-old boy in a West Coast detention center—"Dear Teacher, My name is A_____ and I am in the ninth grade and I need some help in my reading. The reason I don't know how to read is that I never went to school too much, and I have problems with my math in school too. I was going to be a dropout until I met you to teach me how to read."

A mother came for help to a family center started by an NCJW Section in the Southwest. Her husband had left her and their three children and she was still reeling from the shock. Even though the family owned their house and the mother had a steady job, the emotional crisis seemed overwhelming. The mother couldn't sleep at night, the children kept asking about their father and begging for his return. She felt she could not handle the sudden responsibilities of a single parent. Referrals were made for counseling and the mother was introduced to Parents Without Partners. A Big Brother was assigned to the oldest child, a nine-year-old boy, and teachers at a day care center helped the younger ones. Each week, a volunteer family consultant spent time with the mother, making practical suggestions, offering psychological support, listening, and helping her sort out her feelings toward her husband. Gradually, the mother took hold of her new situation and the emotional climate in the home improved. As noted by an observer: "The mother proved to herself that she can provide for herself and her children, not only financially, but emotionally as well."

In Maryland, a Council volunteer opened her home as a shelter and foster placement to teenage girls, who would otherwise be in a locked detention center. In a letter indicating the complexities of her role, she writes:

We have won a court fight to keep S_____, a 16-year-old runaway as a foster child. She will be with us till she is 18 . . . S_____, who cut most of her classes last year (and failed) came to us with the idea of going to school for three periods and working the rest of the time. When she was shown her aptitude tests and realized that going to school full-time next year would mean that she could make a good living for herself, she decided that she would go full-time and would cut no classes. We gave her a choice—it was her decision—and am I proud! . . . This month will mark our second anniversary as shelter care parents. It is the most rewarding work we've ever done. I get tired sometimes and say I'm going to take a vacation and then the phone rings and the social worker tells me another sad tale about a kid in trouble and I'm hooked!

In one example after another, the special human dimension emerges. Familiarity with the system of juvenile justice evoked concern; volunteering was not far behind—a giving of self in time, energy, and skill. On one side the volunteer, on the other the child and family in need.

Across the country, NCJW Sections reported that volunteers were needed to offer service in all phases of juvenile justice, particularly in detention facilities, training schools, and probation departments.

In Long Beach, California, where a volunteer tutor program is going full force at the Los Padrinos Juvenile Hall, businesswomen, housewives and teachers are participating. They work on a one-to-one basis with teenagers who are weak in basic skills, particularly reading. Many of the 16- and 17-year-olds they encounter are unable to write, spell or compose a letter.

Working in an informal manner, the volunteer tutors talk to the teenagers about their interests and enter into friendly dialogue. The youngsters, for their part, speak freely of their educational needs and often about themselves as well. By staying in touch with the therapists, the tutors also are helpful in that direction. Noting that most of the tutors are over fifty, the coordinator of volunteers reports: "The children respond very well to the older tutors, express their thanks to them for their help and seem to anticipate their visits."

One Council volunteer told about "Tom, Dick and Harry," each encounter a reminder of how much teenagers in trouble reach out for helping hands. With Tom, aged 16, she started a reading lesson in phonics with a first-grade reader.

When he read a word correctly I unconsciously said, 'Good'. The look on his face was one of indescribable joy. The more words he recognized the more lavish my adjectives of praise and the greater his wonderment. Yet his last words to me at the end of the day were, 'Guess you'll tell my therapist how stupid I am.' Did I build up his ego? I tried.

Dick, 17, asked me to teach him how to write. He knew absolutely nothing about cursive penmanship. After three sessions, like waving a magic wand, he was writing very legibly. But he was being released on the following Monday. At the end of the session he said, 'I'll see you next Monday.' I reminded him of his leaving. He replied, 'I'll see you at nine. I'm not being released until noon.' That day I felt most rewarded.

Harry 17, wanted to learn how to write a letter. He could read his mail but could hardly write and knew nothing about the construction of a letter. We spent quite a few sessions together, and he assured me he was going back to school, buckle down and even try to enter junior college. I sincerely hope he realizes his ambitions.

At the end of each day I leave the institution with a feeling of contentment. I have not solved anyone's problems, but I have brought a bit of sunshine into the day of a troubled youth.

Official enthusiasm for the program was summed up by a letter from the probation director for Los Angeles County. He cited the Council's volunteer program as "noticeably successful", adding: "The consistency of volunteer attendance with the tutorial program reflects genuine care and dedication on the part of the various volunteers and, thereby, has been able to motivate many of our children to a more positive attitude toward learning."

In South Orange, New Jersey, the Essex County Section recognized the need for services to children on a preventive basis. A result was sponsorship of Our House, a drop-in center for teenagers which grew out of concern over drug abuse. At first, parents in South Orange and adjacent Maplewood offered their own homes for meetings with teenagers in hopes of bridging the generation gap. As the meetings outgrew individual homes, the concept of a permanent meeting place and center developed.

The answer was Our House, a three-story building, staffed by an executive director, two resident aides, a part-time secretary, and four staff members. A "must" in the operation, the staff stresses, is the work of trained NCJW volunteers.

The project had to sell itself to the neighborhood which meant weathering crank letters and threatening, anonymous phone calls. Soon, residents realized that instead of "bad kids" and troublesome teenagers, they had good neighbors. The youngsters impressed everyone by the way they kept the building and grounds in shape, and by their exemplary behavior.

Our House programs include open-ended dialogue groups of five to fifty, encompassing both youngsters and adults, an encounter group, private counseling, primal therapy by a practicing therapist who volunteers his time, nutrition and etching classes, and film study.

Here is what adults participating in the project say about it:

Helping Hands

We're a sort of an alternate school. Some of the youngsters we work with can't make it in regular schools. We're in the middle. We're not a school and not a therapeutic community, but we do a little of both. We fill in where the others fail.

What is our main function? Mostly rap sessions—Our House doesn't offer guidance in the pure sense of the word, but we do use services, particularly Family Services. If a kid can't get along at home, we'll rent a room in a private house or send him to stay with other kids.

How does Our House fit into the juvenile justice system? It acts as a deterrent. It's a way to get kids into alternatives. Rapping is a cathartic. We try to keep the kids out of the courts, and we expect to have close relations with courts, juvenile conference committees and social agencies on a mutual referral basis. And we have a hotline where a kid may call day or night.

In four out of five cases, among approximately 500 youngsters who have enrolled in the program so far, we've been highly successful in getting them back into the community mainstream.

We're very proud of the fact that Maplewood's Chief of Police said recently that the project is 'not only doing a fine job, but is absolutely necessary' as an adjunct to dealing with youth problems. And his South Orange counterpart has spoken similarly.

In Dallas County, Texas, the Richardson-Plano Section of NCJW approached the county welfare department with a plan for a Family Outreach Center. The Section took on the responsibility for the funding, except for the salaries of welfare personnel, and Section members became family consultant volunteers. It was not long before a consensus emerged among the volunteers: they were getting more than they were giving.

Since the concept of Family Outreach was new in the county, the Section went about spreading the word that help was available *before* crises developed. Members spoke before PTA groups, civic and church organizations, were interviewed in newspapers and over radio and television, and distributed brochures. Referrals came in from all over the county.

As a volunteer, each woman prepared herself by joining a group of 12 to 14 persons who took a twelve-week training course that included a two-hour weekly session. After that, the group met on an ongoing basis twice a month for 1½ hours with their trainer, a professional volunteering his or her services. The training group itself became a mutually supporting unit, each individual learning from the other, and generating an esprit de corps.

At the Center, once the social worker handles intake, a volunteer is assigned to a family, making an average of two appointments a month. The volunteer also talks to the family on the phone as often as necessary. For each volunteer, her task is basic—to find out what each family needs and to help fill that need.

The Section reported at the two-year mark that the outreach program "has made a very important difference in human lives" in the area. "Numbers do not tell the story, but if imagination can be applied to them, one can understand what it means that as of May 1, 1974, 69 families have been helped by the center and more than 200 children's lives have been changed for the better."

In St. Louis, Council volunteers were sworn in as assistant deputy juvenile officers after completing 60 hours of training. For ten weeks, the volunteers attended three-hour sessions twice a week before being assigned to counsel youngsters referred to them after informal court hearings. "This program is exceptional and very professional," the Section reports. "Women's interest never flagged. In a ten-week training period one could expect some defection or attrition. There was none."

The following letter of approbation was received from the director of special services for St. Louis County Court:

The volunteers provided by the National Council of Jewish Women have demonstrated remarkable ability as Citizen Deputy Juvenile Officers. Individually, they have brought to the Court situation a multiplicity of attitudes, talents, and skills which have served to provide a wider range of treatment for delinquent children. After a year and a half of involvement at the Court, their motivation and interest remains high. With training, they have performed the task of a Citizen Deputy Juvenile Officer in an efficient and productive manner. Our Court staff has not only accepted the contribution of these Citizen Deputy Juvenile Officers, but they have also become dependent on them to help pick up the overload on their individual caseload. By their involvement, the members of the National Council of Jewish Women have demonstrated a constructive way for lay people to become involved in the ever-increasing problem of juvenile delinquency in this country.

In Memphis, NCJW participated in a citizens' board to establish Runaway House, supporting the project by providing, first, seed money and then 50 to 75 NCJW volunteers. In addition, close to 250 citizens from the community as a whole have been trained in the Runaway House program. Council's representative chaired the citizens' board and then became coordinator of volunteers after the house opened. Her reaction: "For me, working with these youngsters has probably been the most rewarding experience of my life."

Runaway House volunteers do everything from planning menus to aiding in counseling, from office work to research and planning, from obtaining arts and crafts supplies to public speaking. All their activities are linked to the House's carefully defined mission of "helping individual teenagers define their relationship to the world around them." It is a place where youngsters have the chance to "get it all together," with the help of a roof over their heads, decent meals, and sympathetic assistance from concerned volunteers and professionals.

In Bridgeport, Connecticut, the local Section sponsored the Mushroom, a creative workshop for girls referred by Juvenile Court. This program was a first step and the Section has moved towards development of a diversion program. A description of the Mushroom offers the flavor and feeling of this type of project. Like so many volunteer efforts, flexibility permitted this service to move in the direction of the children's expressed needs:

The first thing that must be said about the Mushroom is that it has a warm atmosphere. It is inviting, comfortable. There's a lot going on: pictures on the wall, fabrics, materials, paints, macramé boards, food-goodies, toaster, blender, works-in-progress or finished, posters, original Mondrian designs (by the kids), phonographs, records, etc. etc. Furnished with round tables, workbench, plenty of cushions to flop on the floor, and floor-to-ceiling bookcases full of books (studiously avoided), the Mushroom is inviting, the someplace to go, where there is something to do, with somebody who cares. For some, it is a substitute for a home that is no home. Quite often, as in all interaction between people, personality clashes and hostilities erupted, but happily gave rise to such things as mock courts, peer reprimands, and value discussions in their wake. And though the Mushroom is definitely not a therapy or counseling center, I feel strongly that a trusting adult-teen relationship (non-professional in the usual sense) can be as therapeutic as therapy.

In addition to its drop-in, air your gripes, voice your fears, articulate your dreams aspect, the Mushroom has

*been involved in some very real, very instructive (and
structured) activities including the following: painting,
dancing, creative stitchery, glass-staining, gift-wrapping,
beading, macramé, and, on occasion, homework helping.
One of our proudest achievements is the arrangement
whereby four talented girls get five hours a week of art
instruction from an accomplished artist-teacher. Some of
their preliminary efforts were displayed in Washington
at the 1974 NCJW Joint Program Institute, but these
preliminary drawings are as nothing compared with
the oils they have now graduated to.*

In Tacoma, Washington, a job-placement program for youths on probation is one outgrowth of the
volunteer program initiated by NCJW at the juvenile detention center. This aspect of the service involves the
larger community in helping its youth in trouble. Com-
panies donated funds to run large advertisements whose
headlines told the story: WHAT IS A YOUNG PERSON
WORTH TO YOU? . . . THE VOLUNTEER JOB
PLACEMENT SERVICE THINKS HE IS WORTH A
LOT!
The case was presented in ten emphatic statements:

1. Troubled kids cost everyone, in terms of heartache,
ruined lives, as well as money.

2. A job can give a young person new directions, new
goals, new positive feelings about himself.

3. The young people we represent have proven their
reliability, and are eager to work.

4. They are 15-18 years old and need part-time, full-time
or temporary work.

5. We are trying to help them find that work.

6. We need your help.

7. Your help can be an influence that might mark a turning point in a youngster's life.

8. Here is your chance to do something and get a good employee as well.

9. Call us if you have work; or mail in the coupon if you'd like to hear more.

10. Kids are worth a lot, help us give them the chance to see that.

As the volunteer in charge of finding jobs for children in the program says, "I am sort of helping the caseworker, and now I'm asking the community to help me."

The Justice for Children survey in Rochester, New York, suggested that a guide to all the services available to youth in Monroe County was needed. A coalition was formed, spearheaded by Rochester Section, including the Rochester-Monroe County Youth Board and the Psychodiagnostic Laboratory of the University of Rochester School of Medicine. Funding for the project was secured from a number of sources, including a sizeable grant from the Section. Rochester Section described the project as follows:

Our guide will be multi-indexed, and will provide definitive, comprehensive information. It will be made available to all youth-serving professionals, public and private agencies, schools, libraries, and hopefully, physicians. There is currently no publication available that does this. . . . With this guide available, those seeking service—whether they be intake officers of the court or similar personnel in other agencies or parents and school counselors and psychologists—will have at their fingertips all of the possible services available to any particular youth. In addition, we hope to stimulate a higher degree of coordination among the agencies involved, by pointing out weaknesses in certain areas of youth programming.

The result of the project was a hard cover, 200-page book in looseleaf form to make annual updating easy. A chairwoman of the project reports, "We are very excited about our *Guide,* and the generosity of the Rochester community has been overwhelming."

The Justice for Children Chairwoman of Syracuse Section writes of continued activity in the area of juvenile justice:

Under the leadership of NCJW, the Citizens Coalition for Juvenile Justice has been formed. This group is open to all interested people, lay and professional, who wish to act on some of our findings. We have approximately 200 involved and we are working on three major projects:

1. The production of a television program highlighting juvenile justice in Syracuse.

2. Organizing coffees in areas where group homes are proposed so that there will be less neighborhood resistance; also lobbying for planning and zoning boards to pass favorably on these group homes.

3. Helping to improve our family court facilities by studying reallocation of space and providing volunteer babysitting for siblings of those on the court docket.

To date, the work we have done in the past has begun to bring pressure and change. Our family court judges are now sitting in juvenile court for three months instead of one, which was one of the recommendations of our study . . . the detention center has been allocated funds for renovation by the county executive and there is before our county legislature a proposal for upgrading and increasing personnel. Our probation department has begun to reach out into the community and is using increased numbers of volunteers.

These changes seem small, but each one hopefully is a step in the right direction, and as our newspapers continue to point out, we Council women have been the catalyst.

The Justice for Children Chairwoman in Tucson writes, "I visited our juvenile center on Friday and am happy to tell you that the population there is very low. Most of the children are now in group homes and no longer institutionalized." This statement reflects the impressive progress in that community as a result of the efforts of another coalition established by Council women: the Coalition for the Community Treatment of Children. In April, 1973, innovative and controversial programs were being developed by the local county juvenile court center. Juvenile Court Judge Collins sought public support for these programs and awareness of the plight of children in trouble in the county and state; the coalition was a direct response to his appeals. Among the many activities of the coalition was the sponsorship of an "Information Day" for local candidates, designed to find out the candidates' views about juvenile justice and to enlighten them to the principles of community treatment. In a letter to candidates announcing this program, a short history of the coalition, its aims, and its accomplishments, was delineated as follows:

The first nine months of our existence as an organization was devoted to raising the consciousness of the community to a level of awareness necessary to begin to cope with the problem of children in trouble. Our main thrust was to bring the issue of community responsibility for children to the people and to representatives of local government. We rendered support to the local court to the extent that funding was provided to the Court Center to raise staff salaries, to cut the 100 percent turnover every eighteen months. We worked with the city and county to change zoning regulations in order to open group homes within neighborhoods. This was successful to the extent that there are now fourteen group homes operating within the Tucson metropolitan area. A year ago there were none. Staff turnover at the Court Center dropped 80 percent.

By opening these group homes, the commitment rate of children to the Department of Corrections has dropped from 271 in 1972 to 25 last year. By raising community awareness of the problem of children in trouble and the fact that very few are candidates for incarceration, the number of children from this county in institutional placement, including the Department of Corrections, has dropped substantially and, at the same time, recidivism for adjudicated children has dropped 30 percent during 1973.

From jobs in Tacoma to art lessons in Bridgeport, from learning to write a letter in the Long Beach juvenile hall to dropping in at a youth center in South Orange, from the coalition in Tucson to a guide of services in Rochester, the network of help was stretched to meet the needs of young people. Different communities offer different challenges. What has been demonstrated is the important role to be played by the helping hands of volunteers.

8 Reforms and Remedies

Winds of change have begun to influence juvenile justice, and are forcing a new accountability upon the system. Hard questions are being asked: Is crime being deterred? Rehabilitation provided? Society protected?

When NCJW Sections summarized their findings on both legislation and policies, the pattern was clear. Changes are needed in all aspects of the system. The reports cited juvenile court programs as "largely composed of a mixture of precedent, hunch and prejudice," institutions were depicted as imposing "isolation and oppression at an impressionable age," "attention, not detention" was urged, the courtroom was called "the least appropriate place to solve social problems." One report warned that "without the proper facilities to handle the special needs of different types of juvenile offenders, there can be no true juvenile justice."

An overwhelming number of NCJW studies cited the need for policy changes in police departments, the courts, probation, detention and training schools. A large majority saw the need for legislative action to implement the changes.

After studying reports from more than 100 Sections—some covering all phases of the system of juvenile justice, others limited to parts—the NCJW Task Force pinpointed six specific goals involving both policy and legislation. The context in which they were placed was realistic: "The goals set forth are neither revolutionary nor all-inclusive. They address themselves to certain issues that we encountered in many parts of the country and that lend themselves to remedy through enforced legislative and administrative safeguards." The goals were in line with recommendations made by national commissions and recognized authorities. In some states, some are already in practice.

Six steps to Justice for Children embodied in the NCJW handbook, *Children's Rights*, are:

1. Status offenders should be removed from the jurisdiction of the judicial system.

2. Representation by counsel should be assured.

3. Detention should be minimized and limited.

4. Children's rights in institutions should be observed and protected.

5. Police and court records should be confidential and expungeable.

6. Waiver to adult criminal court should not be permitted.

The goal of removing status offenders from court jurisdiction is crucial. It involves de-criminalizing "children's crimes," the status offenses applicable only to children. Besides the commonly used charges of truancy, running away and incorrigibility, individual states have added their own variations, which reflect outmoded attitudes rather than speak to the needs of children.

The reasoning behind this recommendation is that the court system is an inappropriate place to handle these types of problems. These children need help, but sending them to court can do more harm than good because it stigmatizes the youngsters and frequently results in commitments which compound rather than solve their problems. Meanwhile, by handling cases they are not equipped to handle and for which they lack resources, the courts are diverted from their proper concern: criminal behavior. Status offenders, whose behavior expresses family or school problems, should receive counseling and other supportive services in their communities, but outside the justice system.

This position parallels that of the Task Force on Juvenile Delinquency of the President's Commission on Law Enforcement and the Administration of Justice. It was reiterated at the White House Conference on Children. The President's Task Force noted that too frequently parents use the courts to evade their own responsibilities and to vent hostility against their children. In reality, the parent—rather than the child—may be the one in trouble.

Or, as noted by a 1973 report of the Massachusetts Committee on Children and Youth, the child may be right to run away. The response may very well be the healthy action to take. "An extraordinary number of children left circumstances that had become overwhelming and intolerable for them; they were both psychologically deprived and physically abused," the report said. "For these children running away seems to be a healthy reaction to an impossible situation."

The confirming irony for the NCJW position is the finding that within the juvenile justice system status offenders do not receive the special treatment that the special designation is supposed to guarantee. Instead, they are often treated more harshly. This was apparent in the NCJW studies and was also documented by the National Advisory Commission on Criminal Justice Standards and Goals. The Commission found that status offenders were much more likely to be detained than seriously delinquent youths and once detained, were twice as likely to be held more than thirty days. Moreover, courts were more likely to order confinement for status offenders—and for average stays that were much longer.

The recommendation that status offenders be kept out of the courts constitutes a challenge to the status quo and to vested interests in the juvenile justice system. One aspect of the change would be closing training schools that are largely populated by status offenders sent there by the courts. In Massachusetts, when all training schools were shut down, much resistance came from personnel within the system. De-criminalizing status offenses also sharply limits the jurisdiction of the juvenile courts, and raises the issue of public accountability of the community resources to which children and families are referred.

NCJW has placed major emphasis upon group homes as alternatives to institutionalization (the subject of the special handbook, *How to Set Up A Group Home).* Group homes are not urged as a substitute for probation but to be "used only for the small proportion of children who *really* need to live away from home." This is only an estimated ten percent of the children brought to juvenile and family courts. "In a good group home," the NCJW Task Force noted, "a child can learn to live independently, to use the best in himself and in what the community has to offer, with the support and guidance of his peers and a few adults in an atmosphere of caring." (One of the first NCJW Sections to respond organized a group home in Teaneck, New Jersey, in coalition with the local Youth Guidance Council. An 11-room, split-level, one-family house was purchased to accommodate up to eight runaway girls.)

The recommendation to remove status offenders from the juvenile justice system reaches deeper. It calls for communities to meet their responsibilities by providing the necessary resources to help troubled children and their families. These include family counseling, special day care and after-school facilities, child guidance centers, school counseling, health services and supportive family services. Unfortunately, in most communities NCJW found that a child must get into trouble with the law before getting help. Thus the corollary recommendation: *that community resources be made available to all children when they need them; an arrest or court record should not be an eligibility requirement.*

While the Gault decision of the Supreme Court established the right of juveniles to legal counsel, both the letter and the spirit of this opinion are being violated. NCJW studies repeatedly found that the offering of legal counsel may be judicial lip service and that the right is being waived without full understanding of the consequences.

The Task Force therefore recommended that *"every child facing the possibility of detention, commitment, restraint of his freedoms, or an increase in such restraint be represented by counsel.* Neither indigence, nor ignorance, nor unwilling parents should deprive the child of this safeguard . . . from the moment he is taken into custody through his release from probation."

Legal services, in whatever form the community provides them, should be designed to permit assignment of the same attorney to represent a child from intake to disposition, with adequate time for preparation (see chapter on *Courts*). Achieving this requires state and federal funds because of the large proportion of indigent children involved. Only by providing these resources can the Gault decision have meaning.

As an experience that traumatizes and stigmatizes children and can even begin their education in crime, detention should be a *last* resort, not a reflex action by authorities. Four major questions are involved: Who decides on detention? By what criteria? For how long? Where?

Since detention is a serious matter involving loss of freedom, the decision should rest with the courts and require a hearing in which the child has legal counsel. Furthermore, to avoid abuses, court personnel authorized to conduct detention hearings must be available 24 hours a day, seven days a week. This alone, according to the National Advisory Commission on Criminal Justice, would reduce the use of detention by at least one-fourth.

The criteria for detaining a child should be both explicit and limiting. Many states specify that children can be detained only where they will injure themselves or others or damage property, or where no other supervision is available or where the child is not likely to appear for court hearings. The National Advisory Commission is more restrictive in its criteria, limiting detention to cases where a child has escaped from an institution or is accused of a physical attack in which the victim required medical treatment.

However, the Commission adds a criterion which strikes a note of preventive detention by including children who have been found delinquent three or more times within the previous year or at least five times within the previous two years. The Task Force believes that such a practice, which is on shaky constitutional grounds for adults, should not be imposed upon children.

Besides the abuses flowing from preventive detention, children may be kept in detention when there is nothing else to do with them. This is an unconscionable substitute for temporary care in a non-secure group or foster home, penalizing children indiscriminately. The only offense involved may be that their parents do not want them at home. These children, ironically, are likely to be kept in detention the longest—as societal problems that are not faced by the community, but hidden when the victims become invisible.

The amount of time in detention should be limited by law to 24 hours if no petition is filed. Adjudicatory and dispositional hearings should be held within 15 days; and post-disposition detention should be limited to 48 hours. The NCJW Task Force stressed that "to find children held for months and even years in detention facilities awaiting placement makes mockery of claims of 'treatment and rehabilitation.' "

Detention centers themselves should be supervised by the states under prescribed standards, and inspected regularly to guarantee that they are providing adequate care and services. Detention of juveniles in adult facilities should be prohibited by law, and that law strictly enforced.*

Plans for new juvenile detention facilities require close scrutiny.** Such facilities invite the assignment of children who do not belong there. Detention facilities too easily become places for holding children instead of developing and using constructive alternatives—such as round-the-clock screening, psychological

---

*Appearing before the Senate Subcommittee on Juvenile Delinquency in 1973, Rosemary Sarri of the National Assessment of Juvenile Corrections testified that approximately 300,000 juveniles are detained in jails each year.

**The importance of public alertness was demonstrated in Louisville, Ky. When the local NCJW and Junior League groups learned of construction plans for a detention facility which they felt was too large and badly situated, they managed to change both aspects by mobilizing community opposition.

Reforms and Remedies

services, family counseling, short-term runaway homes, foster care, and intensive probation.

The rights of children in institutions need protection on two levels. The first level concerns the rules and conditions of confinement. The second concerns the right—not the privilege—to rehabilitation services, as well as educational and medical services. NCJW studies in various parts of the country found that "storage" rather than rehabilitation emerges as the main theme of training schools.

Accordingly, the NCJW Task Force recommended that no more large training schools be constructed and that the existing ones be closed. Such schools suffer from the problems of size and impersonality and present a persistent pattern of abuses that is difficult to monitor and to correct. The alternative lies in small community-based facilities, such as group homes, to which leading figures in the corrections field are turning.

Until this can be accomplished, the pain of punishment by incarceration in training schools should be kept under control. Thus:

Solitary confinement and similar punishments should be abolished.

Physical punishment must not be tolerated.

Such practices as confiscation and censorship of mail, compulsory haircuts; obligatory wearing of uniforms and other practices which treat children as convicts, should be ended.

Strict limits should be placed on use of behavior-modifying drugs. They should be administered only on written authorization of an examining physician, supported by his written diagnosis, and specifying a time limit. The decision to use them should be subject to appeal.

Initial commitment to an institution should be based on the availability of treatment and services to meet a youngster's needs. It is deceptive and destructive to send a child away for a program of treatment that he or she will not receive. The court's order should specify the treatment program and provide for periodic progress reports. A child's attorney or an appropriate independent agency should be empowered to observe and evaluate the program in terms of the court's order and the child's changing needs.

Children should not be branded for life if they have come into contact with the juvenile justice system. To avoid imposing this unwarranted and enduring punishment on children, police and court records should be confidential in the first place, and provision made for their expungement.

NCJW studies found that even where police and court records are supposed to be confidential, they are made available to the armed forces, prospective employers, colleges and civil service agencies. Legislative safeguards on confidentiality must be backed up by enforcement. Thus the recommendation: *that police and court records be open only to the judge and court professional staff involved in the case, the child's attorney and parents or guardians, and any agency given custody of the child.* Records should be made available to police in other jurisdictions only by subpoena and to researchers only when anonymity of the child is assured.

Furthermore, statutes should clearly establish that a person taken into custody as a child may truthfully answer on any official form that he has never been arrested. That is the intent of the technicality, "taken into custody"—to avoid a permanent stigma. The NCJW Task Force was particularly concerned about including juvenile records in adult files and their submission to centralized criminal files. Such practices are particularly insidious and at odds with the rehabilitative philosophy of juvenile justice.

Expungement of all court and police records should be automatic when a petition is withdrawn or the case dismissed. Where a child has been judged delinquent, expungement should be available within two years of release or supervision, provided there has been no further adjudication. The child, the family and the attorney should be notified of this right upon the child's release.

In many states, juvenile courts can waive jurisdiction to adult criminal courts, depending on the seriousness of the charge and the child's age and previous record. The juvenile court decides what is "in the best interest" of the community and whether the child is "amenable to treatment and rehabilitation." Public attitudes also figure in a decision that can be highly subjective, even arbitrary.

Instead, the NCJW Task Force recommends that *the system of waiver from juvenile court to adult criminal court be abolished.* Having set an upper age limit for juveniles, the state should abide by it in keeping with the concept of juvenile court based on rehabilitation. Noting its recommendation that status offenders be removed from court jurisdiction, the Task Force points out that this would permit the justice system to concentrate its resources on its appropriate concern—those children who have committed serious crimes.

As long as the system of waiving jurisdiction from juvenile court persists, legal safeguards should be scrupulously maintained as set forth by the Kent Decision of the Supreme Court. These involve a hearing with counsel after proper notice, access by the child's attorney to investigation reports, and written findings by the court to support a waiver decision. Furthermore, immediate appeal should be available.

As a corollary to these six goals, the overwhelming consensus of Sections was that more money and an increase in adequately trained staff are needed across the board in the system of juvenile justice. The proportion of Sections citing the need for more money ranged from 79 percent in regard to corrections services to 95 percent for probation. The proportion citing the need for more adequately trained staff ranged from 77 percent for training schools to 89 percent for detention.

In state after state Sections began to seek legislative change to correct situations they had discovered. The actions taken included dissemination of information, circulating petitions and issuing calls to action, testimony before legislatures, and meetings with legislators. In several states, NCJW members served on committees studying state juvenile codes, particularly in coalition with other organizations.

Since the national and statewide distribution of NCJW Sections was well-suited to dealing with the fragmentation of the system, action was possible across a wide front. The situation in California—as depicted by California Youth Authority's Director, Allen F. Breed—reflects the situation in other states: "First, there are the State Departments of Youth Authority and Corrections. There are 58 counties with separate probation departments, county jails, juvenile halls, camps, ranches and schools, and a host of private residential facilities. In addition, hundreds of programs are being carried on at the community level by both public and private agencies to rehabilitate offenders and to divert young people from the juvenile justice system. Yet, despite the fact that all of these programs seek to reduce crime and delinquency, there is very little coordination among them." In California, as in other states, an effort to bring about greater unity and coordination has been undertaken on the state level.

Reforms and Remedies

The same problem has existed on the federal level, with a multitude of federal agencies working on the needs of children. A milestone in the attempt to deal with this was reached with the enactment of the Juvenile Justice and Delinquency Prevention Act of 1974. This legislation was the result of years of effort by many concerned organizations and a group of dedicated Congressmen led by Senators Birch Bayh (Ind.) and Marlow Cook (Ky.), and Representatives Augustus Hawkins (Cal.) and Tom Railsback (Ill.).*

The Act emphasizes community-based programs and services, encouraging prevention and diversion. It also provides for establishment of a national training and research institute, certain basic procedural rights, and the development of national guidelines and standards.

It is still too early to gauge the effect of this new legislation, a major step towards coordinating federal efforts, providing impetus for state and local efforts, and centralizing accountability.

Another pressing matter requiring action on the federal level concerns juvenile records. Since an increasing number of states are linked to the federal criminal data bank, expunging local records is ineffective if the same records remain intact in Washington and are open to law enforcement agencies through the country. This is particularly disturbing since the existence of juvenile police records may invest with significance information with little or no relevance.

---

*While action on the bill was pending, Representatives Hawkins and Bell (Cal.) visited one of Los Angeles Section's group homes. Afterwards, one of the girls living there wrote: "When the congressmen and their aides were here I felt very important because if the bill really does get passed and they are able to get more homes set up like this it will really be good for kids who need it. I felt I really did something for all the kids who don't have any parents and who don't have anyone to care for them and love them. I think it is really nice that somebody in this world cares enough to do this sort of thing."

In 1970, the White House Conference on Children reported: "If present trends continue, one out of every nine youngsters will appear before a juvenile court before age 18." The Senate Subcommittee on Juvenile Delinquency estimates that juvenile crime now costs society about $4 billion each year. Although the human cost to children and society cannot be calculated, the price is clearly too high to pay without protest.

Whether the focus is federal, state or local, the central concern remains children. So does the central neglect. That children in this child-centered society are systematically neglected, mistreated and abused, is a disquieting irony. Society gets the system of justice it deserves. The lessons of NCJW's Justice for Children study unmistakably confirm that primary responsibility for solutions rests with the community.

We are instructed in Deuteronomy: "Justice, justice shalt thou pursue." The National Council of Jewish Women is continuing its pursuit in towns and cities from coast to coast. But the goal is too big for the small number of organizations similarly engaged.

A poem posted on the wall of a detention center is titled "Nobody Promised You Tomorrow." We make that promise when we bring children into the world. Who will keep it?

Appendix A

Sections and Units of the
National Council of Jewish Women
Involved in the Justice for Children Program

ALABAMA
Birmingham
Mobile
Selma
ARIZONA
Tucson
CALIFORNIA
Contra Costa
East Bay
Long Beach
Los Angeles
Marin
North Orange County
Orange Coast
Palo Alto
Sacramento
San Francisco
San Gabriel Valley
COLORADO
Denver
CONNECTICUT
Greater Bridgeport
Greater Danbury
Greater Hartford
Norwalk
DELAWARE
Wilmington
DISTRICT OF COLUMBIA
Washington
FLORIDA
Greater Miami
Hollywood
Jacksonville
Orlando

Tampa
St. Petersburg
GEORGIA
Atlanta
Savannah
ILLINOIS
Chicago
North Shore
Northwest Suburban
South Cook
West Valley
INDIANA
Indianapolis
KENTUCKY
Louisville
LOUISIANA
Greater New Orleans
Shreveport
MARYLAND
Baltimore
Frederick
Howard County
Montgomery County
MASSACHUSETTS
Greater Boston
New Bedford
Springfield
Worcester
MICHIGAN
Greater Detroit
MINNESOTA
Minneapolis
St. Paul
MISSOURI

Greater Kansas City
St. Louis
NEBRASKA
Omaha
NEW JERSEY
Bayonne-Jersey City
Bayshore
Burlington County
Camden County
Essex County
Fairlawn
Greater Elizabeth
Greater Plainfield
Greater Red Bank
Greater Summit
Greater Westfield
Mid-Bergen
Middlesex County
Northern Valley
Passaic-Clifton
Paterson
Somerville
Teaneck
NEW YORK
Brooklyn
Buffalo
Huntington
New York
North Country
Northern Westchester
Orangetown
Lakeville
Peninsula
Rochester
Rockland County
Roslyn
South Shore
Syracuse
NORTH CAROLINA
Asheville
Greensboro
OHIO
Akron
Cincinnati
Cleveland

Columbus
Toledo
Youngstown
OKLAHOMA
Oklahoma City
Tulsa
OREGON
Portland
PENNSYLVANIA
Erie
Harrisburg
Greater Philadelphia
Pittsburgh
Shenango Valley
Wilkes-Barre
RHODE ISLAND
Providence
SOUTH CAROLINA
Charleston
Greenville
TENNESSEE
Memphis
Nashville
TEXAS
Greater Dallas
El Paso
Fort Worth
Houston
Irving
Richardson-Plano
San Antonio
UTAH
Salt Lake City
VIRGINIA
Hampton Roads
Norfolk
Northern Virginia
Richmond
WASHINGTON
Seattle
Tacoma
WEST VIRGINIA
Charleston
WISCONSIN
Milwaukee

Appendix B

Section and Unit Projects by Category

SERVICES IN COOPERATION WITH PROBATION DEPARTMENTS

Bayonne-Jersey City, New Jersey
Camden County, New Jersey
El Paso, Texas
Greater Bridgeport, Connecticut
Greater Westfield, New Jersey
Louisville, Kentucky
Tacoma, Washington
Wilmington, Delaware

PREVENTATIVE AND COUNSELING SERVICES

Birmingham, Alabama
Essex County, New Jersey
Harrisburg, Pennsylvania
Irving, Texas
Los Angeles, California
Memphis, Tennessee
Norfolk, Virginia
North Shore, Illinois
Northern Westchester, New York
Portland, Oregon
Richardson-Plano, Texas
Roslyn, New York
St. Louis, Missouri

RUNAWAY HOMES • GROUP HOMES • FOSTER CARE

Columbus, Ohio
Fort Worth, Texas
Greater Miami, Florida
Hampton Roads, Virginia
Houston, Texas
Lakeville, New York
Los Angeles, California
Memphis, Tennessee
Montgomery County, Maryland
Nassau County, New York
Oklahoma City, Oklahoma
Orangetown, New York
Rochester, New York
Salt Lake City, Utah
Shreveport, Louisiana
St. Louis, Missouri
Syracuse, New York
Teaneck, New Jersey

COURT-RELATED PROGRAMS

Bergen County, New Jersey
Cleveland, Ohio
Cook County, Illinois
Erie, Pennsylvania
Greater Miami, Florida

New Orleans, Louisiana
New York City, New York
Pittsburgh, Pennsylvania
St. Louis, Missouri
Syracuse, New York

SERVICES TO CHILDREN IN INSTITUTIONS

Bayonne-Jersey City, New
  Jersey
Camden County, New Jersey
East Bay, California
Greater Hartford, Connecticut
Greater Kansas City, Missouri
Hampton Roads, Virginia
Houston, Texas
Long Beach, California
Montgomery County, Maryland
North Country, New York

North Shore, Illinois
Northern Westchester, New
  York
Orangetown, New York
Portland, Oregon
San Gabriel Valley, California
Selma, Alabama
South Shore, New York
St. Louis, Missouri
Tacoma, Washington

PUBLIC AFFAIRS ACTIVITIES

Atlanta, Georgia
Baltimore, Maryland
Denver, Colorado
Greater Dallas, Texas
Greater Elizabeth, New Jersey
Greater Miami, Florida
Los Angeles, California
Louisville, Kentucky
North Shore, Illinois
Pittsburgh, Pennsylvania

Portland, Oregon
Richmond, Virginia
San Antonio, Texas
Savannah, Georgia
Seattle, Washington
Springfield, Massachusetts
St. Louis, Missouri
Tacoma, Washington
Tucson, Arizona

COMMUNITY EDUCATION PROGRAMS

Atlanta, Georgia
Burlington County, New
  Jersey

Essex County, New Jersey
Greater Dallas, Texas
Greater Hartford, Connecticut

Greater Miami, Florida
Greater Red Bank, New Jersey
Greater Westfield, New Jersey
Greensboro, North Carolina
Houston, Texas
Jacksonville, Florida
Louisville, Kentucky
Marin, California
Nassau County, New York
Northern Westchester, New York

Palo Alto, California
Pittsburgh, Pennsylvania
Portland, Oregon
Richmond, Virginia
Rochester, New York
Sacramento, California
Savannah, Georgia
Somerville, New Jersey
St. Louis, Missouri
Syracuse, New York
Toledo, Ohio

JUSTICE FOR CHILDREN COALITION EFFORTS

Atlanta, Georgia
Bergen County, New Jersey
Cleveland, Ohio
Denver, Colorado
Erie, Pennsylvania
Essex County, New Jersey
Greater Bridgeport, Connecticut
Greater Dallas, Texas
Greater Hartford, Connecticut
Greater Kansas City, Missouri
Greater Red Bank, New Jersey
Greensboro, North Carolina
Louisville, Kentucky

Nassau County, New York
North Country, New York
Palo Alto, California
Rochester, New York
Sacramento, California
San Antonio, Texas
San Francisco, California
Savannah, Georgia
Springfield, Massachusetts
St. Louis, Missouri
Tacoma, Washington
Teaneck, New Jersey
Toledo, Ohio
Tucson, Arizona
Wilkes-Barre, Pennsylvania

NCJW STATE PUBLIC AFFAIRS COMMITTEES
REPORTING ACTION ON
JUSTICE FOR CHILDREN

Alabama	Kansas	Ohio
Arizona	Kentucky	Oregon
California	Louisiana	Pennsylvania
Colorado	Maryland	Tennessee
Connecticut	Massachusetts	Texas
Florida	Minnesota	Utah
Georgia	Missouri	Virginia
Illinois	New Jersey	West Virginia
Indiana	New York	Wisconsin

143

Appendix C

Section and Unit Projects by State

ALABAMA

BIRMINGHAM sponsors Civic Safari, a prevention project; conducts tours of City Hall and police stations to foster positive attitudes towards city officials.

MONTGOMERY provides services to residents of a children's home.

SELMA provides recreational supplies for a regional detention center.

ARIZONA

TUCSON organized a community-wide organization, Coalition for the Community Treatment of Children, which is both supporting funding of community-based programs and sponsoring legislation; Section member on the board of community family counseling program.

CALIFORNIA

EAST BAY sponsored an art fair of work of children in a detention center: provides tutorial and other services to the detention center.

LONG BEACH coordinates a variety of volunteer services in the detention center; also provides tutoring to adolescents on probation in a day center.

LOS ANGELES sponsors El Nido Lodges, three residential treatment homes for adolescent girls; contracts with Los Angeles County Sheriff's Department to provide diversionary counseling service for juveniles picked up by police.

MARIN is gathering information on local laws and procedures of juvenile court, police and probation departments.

PALO ALTO sponsored a public symposium on juvenile justice in coalition with other community organizations.

SACRAMENTO sponsored a public meeting on juvenile justice in cooperation with other member organizations of Women In Community Service.

SAN FRANCISCO cooperated in community study with Junior League and WICS; coalition now attempting to respond to community need for a drop-in center at the Junior High level.

SAN GABRIEL VALLEY provides services to children in the local detention center.

COLORADO

DENVER is involved in legislative activity regarding the state juvenile codes; represented on joint planning committee for statewide advocacy system for youth.

CONNECTICUT

GREATER BRIDGEPORT provides a cultural enrichment program in cooperation with Junior League for adolescent girls on probation; investigating diversion project in cooperation with probation department.

GREATER HARTFORD published and distributed *Justice for Children: Connecticut Report;* received the statewide G. Fox Award for the report; used award funds to purchase equipment for local institutions and homes and for second report; Section working in local detention home and with various state and local agencies on further studies; active in community education; with Junior League, convened a Justice for Children coalition; Section members appointed to many state and local boards working for improvement of services for children.

DELAWARE

WILMINGTON volunteers are working in Probation Department of Family Court.

FLORIDA

GREATER MIAMI published and distributed results of the Justice for Children survey; initiated Juvenile Aide and Referral Service—an in-depth court volunteer program; sponsors a group foster home; involved in legislative activity for civil liberties of juveniles.

JACKSONVILLE members helped form and serve on the city's Youth Service Bureau; the Section's Justice for Children survey was incorporated into an overall study of the Goals and Priorities for the city.

GEORGIA

ATLANTA is active in community education and legislative activity; sponsored a state-wide forum on juvenile justice in conjunction with other community and professional agencies; represented on all committees of the State Crime Commission.

SAVANNAH secured a full-time juvenile court judge through coalition efforts with League of Women Voters; testified before community group interested in correction reform; cooperated in securing grant for Youth Service Bureau.

ILLINOIS

GREATER CHICAGO is working with Sections in the area in a multifaceted volunteer service to the Juvenile Court of Cook County.

NORTH SHORE has worked at the request of a state representative on a bill for a community crisis intervention center; donates Thrift Shop clothes to an institution; helped to establish the Youth Employment Service many years ago; cooperates with other Sections in volunteer service to the Juvenile Court of Cook County.

KENTUCKY

LOUISVILLE worked in coalition with Junior League in community education and social action, especially with regard to the building of an unnecessary detention facility; volunteers in probation project.

LOUISIANA

GREATER NEW ORLEANS provides volunteers for Orleans Parish Juvenile Court.

SHREVEPORT furnished a room in a home for pre-delinquent girls.

MARYLAND

BALTIMORE has testified on several issues relating to Justice for Children.

FREDERICK is sponsoring a group home for boys.

MONTGOMERY COUNTY provides an arts and crafts program at a shelter; donates equipment to halfway house for juvenile drug addicts; compiled a handbook for shelter and foster parents; establishing a network of short-term foster homes.

MASSACHUSETTS

SPRINGFIELD is working on legislative matters; hopes to form local coalition.

MISSOURI

GREATER KANSAS CITY provides service to children in a detention center and vocational school; represented on county task force; working to establish local coalition.

ST. LOUIS started a program utilizing volunteers as deputy juvenile officers; provides services in detention center and group homes; publishes Help posters and cards listing existing services agencies; helped to finance a mini bus used in one local community to bring services to juveniles in need; participates in legislative coalition.

NEW JERSEY

BAYONNE-JERSEY CITY participates in volunteers in probation; provides holiday gifts for children in a detention center.

BURLINGTON COUNTY received the Club of the Year award from the local newspaper for community education on the basis of the survey.

CAMDEN COUNTY works as volunteer probation officers; coordinates volunteer activities at a local shelter; represented on local advisory boards.

ESSEX COUNTY is a cooperating agency of Our House, a multi-service center for teenagers; exploring possible affiliation with county government in establishment of a group home; developed and presented a Justice for Children forum in a municipal courtroom for high school students; convenor and sponsor of other community education efforts.

GREATER ELIZABETH is active in legislative activity.

GREATER RED BANK is active in a coalition of organizations which sponsor community conferences and sponsors a group home for boys.

GREATER WESTFIELD co-sponsored a community forum on Justice for Children; working with the probation department as casework aides.

SOMERVILLE co-sponsored a community forum on Justice for Children.

TEANECK cooperated with other Bergen County Sections in a court aides program; co-sponsors group home for runaway girls.

NEW YORK

BROOKLYN participated in a court survey project in cooperation with the Family Court.

LAKEVILLE supports local group homes.

NEW YORK CITY participated in a court survey project in cooperation with Family Court.

NORTH COUNTRY is exploring funding for a group home; formed child advocacy coalition; provided volunteer services at local state hospital.

NORTHERN WESTCHESTER co-sponsored community forums; provided volunteers to county office of child services.

ORANGETOWN provides services to a foster group home; represented on Youth Service Bureau.

PENINSULA is investigating the problem of child abuse.

ROCHESTER is supporting local group homes; working in coalition to compile, fund and distribute a city-county Youth Services Guide.

ROCKLAND COUNTY is represented on the Youth Service Bureau; considering service to a group home.

ROSLYN sponsors a walk-in center for adolescents.

SOUTH SHORE gives volunteer services to children in the county shelter.

SYRACUSE provided community education via public forum and newspaper series; organized citizens coalition; supporting group homes; providing services to family court.

NORTH CAROLINA

GREENSBORO is working in coalition to set up two program-oriented group homes; will provide financial and volunteer support; organized speakers bureau in area of child abuse.

OHIO

AKRON is represented on boards of local youth-serving agencies.

CLEVELAND is investigating the feasibility of a group home project; convened and organized broad-based Coalition on Juvenile Justice, which has a court-watching project.

COLUMBUS provides volunteer services to a boys' group home.

TOLEDO is working as part of a broad-based coalition planning a week-long meeting on Crime and Prevention with the Regional Planning Unit.

OKLAHOMA

OKLAHOMA CITY is represented on the board of a group home for girls and has provided furniture and volunteer services.

OREGON

PORTLAND provides volunteer services in a youth counseling center; represented on board and planning volunteer program in another counseling center; appointed to a committee to advise policy in use of juvenile records.

PENNSYLVANIA

ERIE was among the founders of Resources for Youth which functions as an advisory committee to the Juvenile Court in finding community-based treatment or placement.

HARRISBURG co-sponsors Youth Scene, a youth and family counseling center for families in a specified geographic area who were not being served by existing agencies.

PITTSBURGH is active in legislation and community education; has written a proposal for a Big Sister Project; provides volunteers to recreation program sponsored by the Juvenile Court; co-sponsored Resident Youth Corps, a delinquency prevention program.

WILKES-BARRE is working as part of a coalition to set up a Council for Juvenile Justice.

RHODE ISLAND

PROVIDENCE is investigating the feasibility of a group home project.

SOUTH CAROLINA

CHARLESTON provides volunteers to Project Happy, a juvenile delinquency prevention project.

TENNESSEE

MEMPHIS sponsors and provides volunteer services to Runaway House, a short-term residence; established a day-care center in response to the findings that many adolescent youngsters were truant because of responsibilities for younger siblings; represented on board of a local agency.

NASHVILLE is cooperating in a local group home project.

TEXAS

EL PASO sponsored summer field trips for juveniles on probation.

FORT WORTH co-sponsors a group home for adolescents.

GREATER DALLAS is active in community education via a seminar (co-sponsored with eight organizations), speaking to other groups and newspaper articles; worked on legislative proposals; looking into feasibility of group home; Section representation on the board of an agency of the Jewish Family Service.

HOUSTON is providing aid to a halfway house; active in community education; exploring volunteer possibilities with juvenile Probation Department; represented on local Child Care Council; co-sponsors Family Outreach Center.

RICHARDSON-PLANO sponsors and provides service to a drop-in center for children and families located in a shopping center.

SAN ANTONIO works in coalition on juvenile justice legislation and on renovation of boys' halfway house.

UTAH

SALT LAKE CITY is represented on the board of the only girls' group home in the city.

VIRGINIA

HAMPTON ROADS provides volunteer service in a detention facility; represented on the board of a local agency.

NORFOLK is represented on the board of a local delinquency prevention agency.

RICHMOND is active in community education and working on legislative proposals.

WASHINGTON

SEATTLE is working to improve the state juvenile code.

TACOMA provides a multi-service volunteer program to dependent and delinquent children at a detention center; works with juveniles on probation under supervision of the Probation Department; serves on board of new Youth Service Bureau; working to improve state juvenile code.

Grateful acknowledgment is made to the Greater New Orleans and Portland, Oregon Sections of NCJW for their generous gifts which made possible the publication of this report.